California
Bar
Examination

Performance Tests
and
Selected Answers

July 2012

PERFORMANCE TESTS AND SELECTED ANSWERS
JULY 2012
CALIFORNIA BAR EXAMINATION

This publication contains two performance tests from the July 2012 California Bar Examination and two selected answers to each test.

The answers received good grades and were written by applicants who passed the examination. The answers were produced as submitted, except that minor corrections in spelling and punctuation were made for ease in reading. The answers are reproduced here with the consent of their authors.

<u>Contents</u>

Performance Test A

INSTRUCTIONS AND FILE

IN RE CLEF, INC.

IN RE CLEF, INC.
INSTRUCTIONS

1. You will have three hours to complete this session of the examination. This performance test is designed to evaluate your ability to handle a select number of legal authorities in the context of a factual problem involving a client.

2. The problem is set in the fictional State of Columbia, one of the United States.

3. You will have two sets of materials with which to work: a File and a Library.

4. The File contains factual materials about your case. The first document is a memorandum containing the instructions for the tasks you are to complete.

5. The Library contains the legal authorities needed to complete the tasks. The case reports may be real, modified, or written solely for the purpose of this performance test. If the cases appear familiar to you, do not assume that they are precisely the same as you have read before. Read each thoroughly, as if it were new to you. You should assume that cases were decided in the jurisdictions and on the dates shown. In citing cases from the Library, you may use abbreviations and omit page citations.

6. You should concentrate on the materials provided, but you should also bring to bear on the problem your general knowledge of the law. What you have learned in law school and elsewhere provides the general background for analyzing the problem; the File and Library provide the specific materials with which you must work.

7. Although there are no restrictions on how you apportion your time, you should probably allocate at least 90 minutes to reading and organizing before you begin preparing your response.

8. Your response will be graded on its compliance with instructions and on its content, thoroughness, and organization.

CRESPI, DONOHO and WAN, PA

9800 Commercial Boulevard

Suite 1000

Cooper City, Columbia 55155

CDWLaw@homepage.com

TO: Applicant

FROM: Luan Wan

RE: CLEF, Inc. – Corporate Governance Review

David Conway, a law school classmate, recently became the Chief Executive Officer (CEO) of the College Loan Equity Fund, Inc. (CLEF), a nonprofit corporation organized under the Columbia Nonprofit Corporation Act. As his first task, Conway is reviewing CLEF's corporate governance practices. He had become concerned about CLEF's practices in the course of interviewing for his new position. His concern has been heightened by a recent Columbia Supreme Court decision dissolving a high-profile nonprofit and by an even more recent announcement by the Columbia Attorney General of an intent to propose legislation to apply principles from the federal Sarbanes-Oxley Act to Columbia nonprofits. On behalf of CLEF, Conway has engaged our firm to conduct an analysis of certain aspects of the company's corporate governance procedures in light of the Smith case and the Attorney General's proposed legislation and, if warranted, suggest modifications to current practices.

Please prepare a memo that presents an objective analysis of whether the following actions violate Columbia law or the Attorney General's proposed requirements:

1. Engagement of an outside accountant;
2. Execution of a lease of corporate facilities;
3. Purchase of corporate insurance;
4. Guaranty of the mortgage of the former CEO; and
5. Failure to share an internal report with the Board of Directors and with loan fund
6. investors.

Excerpt from CLEF's Web Site

http://www.CLEF.org/home/history

What is College Loan Equity Fund?

College Loan Equity Fund, better known as CLEF, is a nonprofit student loan program. The mission of other lenders is to generate equity for their shareholders; ours is to provide education financing to the broadest range of eligible undergraduate students. Our sole charge is to ensure that students have access to affordable funding for their education. We focus on the Humanist Group of colleges that constitute our membership and hundreds of non-member undergraduate schools.

Our History

CLEF, Inc. was formed by Melvin Metzger in 1997 and funded by a $10 million gift from the Metzger Family Foundation. CLEF's initial goal was to make low interest loans to needy undergraduate students who attended one of the 33 small, liberal arts colleges that make up the Humanist Group. These member colleges agreed to extend tuition and attendance discounts for students who qualified for CLEF loans.

CLEF is now a $5 billion nonprofit corporation with virtually all of its assets in the form of promissory notes on the loans it has made to thousands of undergraduate students. Although it has become the largest not-for-profit in the student loan field, CLEF's goal is still the same: to provide greater access to affordable undergraduate financing, and greater access to the information that can help students borrow wisely, manage debt responsibly, and repay their student loans successfully. And CLEF continues to make those below-market-rate loans to especially needy students who attend a Humanist Group college.

INTERVIEW: DAVID CONWAY, CEO, CLEF, INC.

LUAN WAN: David! It's great to see you. What's it been, eight years or so?

DAVID CONWAY: About that, Luan. It was our fifth law school reunion. I missed the tenth.

WAN: It's great to have you back in the area. Tell me about your new position with CLEF.

CONWAY: Well, it's a real opportunity. As you know, I took over as CEO after spending nine years with United American National Bank, initially as Associate General Counsel for its student loan division and then as VP of the division's operations. United American is one of the top lenders to undergraduate students, right behind Sallie Mae and CitiBank. CLEF, on the other hand, is the fastest growing lender in the undergraduate market and number one among the nonprofits in the field. Even so, with a shade over 100 employees, we're a small operation in comparison to the major players in the student loan industry.

WAN: What can we do to be of assistance? By the way, do you mind if we tape this session?

CONWAY: Of course not; go right ahead. As the new CEO I'm feeling my way around, poking into things to learn more about the company. When the Columbia Supreme Court came down with the <u>Smith</u> decision last month it caused me to review the operation of our Board of Directors. Then last week the Attorney General (AG) announced that he intended to propose legislation that will apply key principles of the federal Sarbanes-Oxley Act to Columbia nonprofits. I'm now worried that some of CLEF's long-time Board practices are out of sync with present Columbia law and the new regulations will be even tighter if, as is expected, the legislature adopts the AG's proposal.

WAN: Our firm does a lot of work for Columbia corporations so we have a good handle on local law. We don't do much with nonprofits but I know the Columbia Nonprofit Corporation Code tracks the State's for-profit corporate principles.

CONWAY: That's what I thought. It also makes sense for us to anticipate how current Board procedures fit with the Attorney General's efforts to extend key rules from the federal Sarbanes-Oxley law to Columbia nonprofits. As I see it, up-front planning is critical.

WAN: I thought that Sarbanes-Oxley only applies to for-profit public corporations?

CONWAY: You're correct; most SOX provisions are limited to for-profits. But the chatter among corporate counsel and the nonprofit community is about extending SOX 'best practices' to the nonprofit world.

WAN: SOX and 'best practices'?

CONWAY: Oh, sorry. SOX is short for Sarbanes-Oxley and 'best practices' means that the new federal governance and auditing rules have established a standard that many believe nonprofits should or will be forced to adopt. That appears to be the motivation of the Columbia AG — to prevent the possibility of an Enron-type scandal in the nonprofit sector by applying selected SOX principles.

WAN: OK, let's focus on your concerns about CLEF's existing Board practices. I read background info on the company's homepage so I know a bit more about CLEF and its operations. Pretty impressive — a $5 billion nonprofit company.

CONWAY: Yeah, it is amazing that CLEF began as a 'Mom and Pop' lender and has grown up to be a player in the tough student loan business. However, certain holdover governance practices from its small time roots are worrying me. For example, it's a strange Board of Directors. Of the 15 directors, five of them are effectively permanent. Although the company founder, Melvin Metzger, and four of his close personal and business friends technically serve three-year terms, they've been on the Board since the company was created about 15 years ago. With unlimited terms, they keep getting reelected by the corporation's members, the presidents of the Humanist colleges. Five directors come from the college financial aid community and the final five are college presidents, at least three of whom must be from the Humanist Group of colleges. The financial aid directors and the presidents serve single staggered terms of three years.

WAN: What's the problem?

CONWAY: Two things. First, there's a high turnover among the members who come from the academic community. The financial aspects of the student loan business are very complicated. There's a steep learning curve so by the time the financial aid types and the college presidents have caught on, they're rotating off the Board. This means they often defer to the five 'permanent' Board directors on key questions. Second, the Board composition means we don't have any truly sophisticated financial types, no one from investment banking or the consumer credit field. These are serious handicaps in today's complex and competitive student loan business.

WAN: Hmmm. I can see the problem.

CONWAY: I'm very concerned this will only get worse unless we do something. Even the most naive new director asks how much Directors and Officers Insurance we provide in case the directors get sued. But in a post-Enron environment, new directors with investment banking or other sophisticated experience in consumer finance certainly will insist on broader and more expensive coverage.

WAN: I see.

CONWAY: Deferral to the permanent directors and the lack of financial sophistication has led to what I believe are some questionable governance traditions at the Board level. For example, CLEF has used a local CPA firm, Metzger Associates, to conduct its financial oversight since the early days of the company.

WAN: Metzger Associates? Any relationship to...?

CONWAY: Yup, Sue Metzger, the principal in Metzger Associates, is Melvin's first cousin. However, if we bring in a national accounting firm and conduct rigorous, in-depth SOX-type audits, it will cost the company twice what we pay Metzger.

WAN: Uh oh, that could create cost-control questions. Anything else?

CONWAY: Two years ago when CLEF added a loan servicing division the number of employees doubled, from about 50 to over 100. The company was forced to find larger quarters and it signed a long-term lease for a vacant department store that was remodeled to accommodate the expanded operations. Bernie Baugh, a member of the CLEF Board and Melvin Metzger's college classmate, is a partner in Center City Realty, the company that owns the property and served as the general contractor for the renovation of the facilities.

WAN: Wasn't that an issue in the <u>Smith</u> decision, questions about 'insider' transactions?

CONWAY: That's one of the reasons I became nervous. In digging around, I also came across a recent internal report authored by the director of strategic planning that forecasts changes in the student loan market that could affect the company's liquidity. The report never was sent to the Board by my predecessor and it wasn't disclosed to potential investors in the last investment offering.

WAN: Can you provide me documentation of these incidents you just described?

CONWAY: I'll fax over a memo I've been working on that outlines what I've found so far. I'm still feeling my way and there may be more. I'd appreciate your analysis about how these actions jibe with Columbia law.

WAN: We'll get something back to you as quickly as possible.

CONWAY: Thanks. I also need your assistance in anticipating the impact of the Attorney General's sketchy proposal to apply some SOX-like rules on Columbia nonprofits. With $5 billion in assets and $150 million in annual revenue, CLEF is exactly the type of nonprofit that is the target of his legislation. Given the somewhat loose governance practices followed in the past, there's no question in my mind that CLEF needs to be alert to the likely stricter financial accountability standards the AG is proposing.

WAN: That seems to make sense, but why do you need us? You're an excellent lawyer and have years of experience in the for-profit student loan field with an organization that is subject to Sarbanes-Oxley. Why don't you review the AG's proposal and make your recommendations directly to the Board?

CONWAY: First, I'm the CEO and I shouldn't act as the company's legal advisor. And, frankly, the situation is fairly delicate. The company has been run like a family foundation pursuing its philanthropic mission. Melvin Metzger, the founder and Board chairman since the company's inception, is passionate about providing financial support to young people seeking an education. He had the financial resources to begin the nonprofit company and the business acumen to alter its operations several times to keep CLEF afloat and greatly expand its reach beyond the original group of students. Unfortunately, Melvin has a very proprietary attitude toward the Company and doesn't recognize that Board practices do not seem to have kept pace with CLEF's rapid transformation from a private foundation to a minor marketing company to a full-fledged financial institution that attracts major international investors and manages a significant loan portfolio. I am committed to making CLEF the model student loan company – profit or nonprofit – by adhering to the highest standards of Board governance and financial operations. But I have to be careful in communicating any criticism about current practices. Sound advice from a qualified objective source, such as your firm, will be better received by Melvin and the Board.

WAN: While I understand you're new and Metzger apparently is set in his ways, isn't it clear to everyone that avoiding potential liability is in the interest of the company and the Board? Assuming good faith on the part of the directors, how can they object to your call for high standards?

CONWAY: Well, the problem in transitioning the company to its new financial and business reality is cultural as much as anything. I'm worried about straining long-standing positive personal relationships among Board members.

WAN: OK, let me take a look at the Columbia Nonprofit Corporation Code, the case handed down by the Supreme Court and the Attorney General's announcement about his intended legislative proposal before making any recommendations for you to take to the CLEF Board. You send me the memo you mentioned and we'll do our very best.

CONWAY: Thanks, Luan.

College Loan Equity Fund, Inc.

Affordable Funding for Undergraduate Education

Box 2004 Cooper City, Columbia 55354

MEMO -- July 18, 2012

TO: Luan Wan, Crespi, Donoho & Wan, P.A.

FROM: David Conway, CEO

RE: <u>CLEF Corporate Governance</u>

As a follow-up to our conversation, the following is information I have gleaned from various CLEF sources. I have attached what I believe to be relevant excerpts from CLEF Board Minutes over the last six years (Attachment A) and the Executive Summary from an internal CLEF report prepared by our Director of Strategic Planning dated six months ago and prior to CLEF's most recent investment offering (Attachment B).

Audit and Financial Issues:

CLEF receives an annual accounting report from Metzger Associates but it doesn't conform to Generally Accepted Accounting Principles (GAAP standards) used by national accounting firms when performing traditional audits of many financial institutions. Although the accounting approach used by Metzger is common when reviewing small and medium size businesses, it does not go into the depth of analysis sophisticated financial institutions usually demand and expect, especially those who regularly seek significant funding from international investors. The Board doesn't have a separate audit committee. In fact, it functions as a committee of the whole for all of its work. For example, an informal executive committee, now composed of Melvin Metzger, Bernie Baugh and Jane Cross but not created by formal Board action, functions on behalf of the Board in the interim between the quarterly meetings.

As I mentioned when we met, CLEF doesn't have a well-balanced and diverse board with a lot of financial savvy. I am concerned the Board doesn't have the expertise to understand complex finance and macroeconomic projections, evaluate accounting recommendations and make generally sound financial decisions to fulfill its fiduciary responsibilities. CLEF's chief financial officer (CFO) leads a generally passive Board through all reviews of Metzger's accounting advice and the complex financial documents the Board has to approve for the annual investor offering process. The CLEF CFO and CEO are always present when Metzger presents any type of report to the Board.

Certification:

The only annual report of a financial nature generated by CLEF is IRS Form 990. Nonprofits under 501(c)(3) do not pay taxes but they must report revenue and expenditures (and any fundraising activity). CLEF's CEO signs off on this report but it doesn't come to the Board for review. My predecessor, Curtis Johnson, the former VP for Financial Aid at Bond College, knew financial aid and student loans but he didn't have an accounting or finance background.

Conflicts of Interest:

CLEF needs to adopt a conflict of interest policy with disclosure standards to guide the board and staff in independent decision-making. Given several of the transactions of the CLEF Board memorialized in the attached Minutes, this is an area about which I have great concern and seek your advice and guidance.

Attachment A

Excerpts from CLEF Board Minutes

October 5, 2011:

Mr. Morgan moved and Ms. Gilmore seconded the reappointment of Metzger Associates as CLEF's certified public accountants. Mr. Morgan noted that this would be the 13th year CLEF has used Metzger Associates as its accounting firm. He mentioned that literally and figuratively Sue Metzger, the cousin of Board Chair Metzger, is a long-standing member of "the CLEF family" and she understands the Company's culture and goals. The motion was adopted unanimously without discussion.

April 14, 2009:

The Board discussed the need to build or lease new facilities to accommodate the expected growth in employees due to the impending creation of a loan servicing division. The CEO and the Board Chairman reported their judgment that the vacant Pomeroy's Department Store in West Cooper City was ideal. With 80,000 square feet and a large parking lot, the property will meet short and long-term projected needs for space. CLEF has been offered $10 per square foot in annual rent for a ten-year term with an option to purchase the property or renew the lease for an additional five years. Renovation estimates run between $800,000 and $1 million, including all furniture. Ms. Metzger from Metzger Associates reported that these figures were within the facilities budget earlier adopted by the Board. On the motion of Ms. Cross, seconded by Mr. Baugh, the Board unanimously (1) approved the lease with Center City Realty; and (2) approved engaging Center City Realty's construction division to serve as the general contractor for the necessary renovations.

October 19, 2007:

The Board took up the matter of the appointment of Curtis Johnson, the VP for Financial Aid at Bond College, as CLEF's CEO for a term of five years. Board Chairman Metzger reported that negotiations were almost complete. One issue remaining was Johnson's need for a mortgage in the amount of $420,000 to purchase a house in Cooper City. Board member Anthony Niedwicki, Executive Vice President of Cooper City Savings, indicated that his bank would make the loan if CLEF would sign as a guarantor. On the motion of Ms. Gilmore, seconded by Mr. Morgan, the Board agreed to guaranty Mr. Johnson's mortgage.

June 15, 2006:

The Board discussed the rising costs associated with various insurance policies required to operate the business. Mr. Metzger reported it would cost almost $95,000 to renew the insurance package with Intercontinental Insurers for the next fiscal year.

Board member John Morgan, a principal in the Cooper City Insurance Consortium, stated he could provide the company with identical coverage at a price at least 10-percent below that quoted for renewal. The Board adopted Ms. Maurer's motion to purchase the necessary insurance from the Cooper City Insurance Consortium.

Attachment B

Excerpt from CLEF Internal Report:

January 21, 2012

TO: Senior Management
FROM: Wendy Sims, Director of Strategic Planning
SUBJECT: Challenges to CLEF's Cash Flow

Executive Summary: Combining the Chief Financial Officer's most recent Company projections and my analysis of the U.S. business climate and college enrollment, I perceive two obstacles to CLEF's short and long-term revenue estimates. First, continued weakness in the white-collar job market nationwide means that fewer college graduates are being employed in high salaried positions. Accepting lower paying jobs means that some graduates will earn less and will have greater difficulty in servicing their loans. Based on CLEF's accumulated data, I estimate that our student loan defaults will slowly rise from six to thirteen percent of the annual loan volume. Complicating the consideration of cash flow is the sharp rise in college graduates entering professional and graduate schools. Medicine, dentistry, law and business are experiencing record applications. A significant shift by college graduates away from the work force and into postgraduate study will mean that undergraduate loans will be deferred for the duration of graduate work. This is likely to result in a dip in CLEF's expected revenue for up to four years. Such a change in revenue may negatively affect our ability to attract investors in our next offering.

Performance Test A

LIBRARY

IN RE CLEF, INC.

LIBRARY

Selected Provisions of Columbia Nonprofit Corporation Code

§ 4830. Performance of Duties by Director of a Nonprofit Corporation; Liability

(1) A director shall perform the duties of a director in good faith, in a manner such director believes to be in the best interests of the nonprofit corporation and its members and with such care, including reasonable inquiry, as an ordinarily prudent person in a like position would use under similar circumstances.

(2) So long as a director acts in good faith, after reasonable inquiry when the need is indicated by the circumstances and without knowledge that would cause such reliance to be unwarranted, a director shall be entitled to rely on information, opinions, reports or statements, including financial statements and other financial data, prepared or presented by any of the following:

      (a) Officers or employees of the corporation the director believes to be reliable and competent in the matters presented;

      (b) Counsel, independent accountants or other persons as to matters the director believes to be within such person's professional or expert competence; or

      (c) A committee of the board upon which the director does not serve, as to matters within its designated authority, which committee the director believes to merit confidence.

(3) A person who performs the duties of a director in accordance with subdivisions (1) and (2) shall have no liability based upon any alleged failure to discharge the person's obligations as a director.

§ 4832. Conflict of Interest Transactions

(1) A conflict of interest transaction is a transaction with the corporation in which a director or officer of the corporation has a direct or indirect interest.

(2) A director or officer has a conflict of interest if, but not only if, another entity in which the director or officer has a material interest is a party to the transaction or another entity of which the director or officer is a director, officer, or trustee is a party to the transaction.

(3) Any conflict of interest transaction is voidable by the corporation, and may be the basis for liability of a director or officer, unless the transaction was fair at the time it was entered into or is approved in accordance with subdivision (4).

(4) A conflict of interest transaction may be approved if:

(a) The material facts of the transaction and the director's or officer's interest were disclosed or known to the board of directors or a committee consisting entirely of members of the board of directors and the board of directors or such committee authorized, approved, or ratified the transaction;

(b) The material facts of the transaction and the director's or officer's interest were disclosed or known to the members and they authorized, approved, or ratified the transaction; or

(c) Approval is obtained from:

(i) The attorney general; or

(ii) A court of record having equity jurisdiction in an action in which the attorney general is joined as a party.

(d) Approval by the board requires the affirmative vote of a majority of the directors who have no direct or indirect interest in the transaction, but no such transaction may be approved by a single member of the board.

(e) Approval meeting the requirements of subdivisions (c) and (d) removes the voidability of the transaction by the corporation and personal liability for directors and officers, but directors so approving must comply with their fiduciary duties in deciding whether to approve.

(f) A director who votes for, assents to or ratifies a transaction made in violation of the Nonprofit Corporation Code and does not comply with standards of conduct established in § 4830 is personally liable to the corporation.

SMITH v. COLUMBIA CHILDREN & FAMILY SERVICES, INC.
Columbia Supreme Court (2012)

The Attorney General filed suit pursuant to Columbia Nonprofit Corporation Code ("Code") to dissolve a nonprofit corporation, Columbia Children and Family Services, Inc. (CCFS). The trial court granted summary judgment for the Attorney General, finding that CCFS had abandoned its charitable purpose and devoted itself to private purposes, and ordered the appointment of a receiver to preserve the remaining corporate assets. CCFS appealed.

The Attorney General maintained that CCFS, a nonprofit, tax-exempt corporation, repeatedly violated the Columbia Nonprofit Corporation Code by: (1) renting property owned by Emily Madison, the sometimes executive director and chairperson of the CCFS board of directors; (2) investing CCFS funds in a local bank in which board members had an interest; and (3) approving transactions that inured to the benefit of the board chairperson and her family and friends.

CCFS's charter of incorporation lists as its purpose: "to provide comprehensive social service for young people who are teenage mothers, handicapped children, underachievers in school and special-problem children." As a nonprofit corporation, CCFS is authorized "to seek public and private funds" to achieve its goals. As it turns out, the Columbia Department of Human Services (DHS) provided almost all of CCFS's funds.[1]

In general terms, a nonprofit is an organization in which no part of the income is distributable to its members, directors or officers. A nonprofit corporation is not prohibited from conducting enterprises for income or from accumulating earnings. However, such revenues must be used for the purposes set forth in the charter. No pecuniary gain can inure to directors or officers and there can be no direct or indirect

---

[1] According to the trial court's finding, more than ninety-nine percent of CCFS's revenue came from DHS. In the three years preceding the Attorney General's action, DHS provided the company with $3.1 million in 2007; $6.8 million in 2008; and $4.9 million in 2009.

distribution of income or profits to them. For example, under § 4858 of the Code, nonprofits are specifically prohibited from lending money to, or guaranteeing the obligation of, a director or officer of the corporation. The bargain made with the government, the taxpayers, and the public in return for benefits such as tax exemption is that the nonprofit will operate for the public good and not for the enrichment of those running it.

Directors and officers of nonprofits, like their for-profit counterparts, owe two basic fiduciary duties to the corporation: the duty of care and the duty of loyalty.

The duty of care imposed on corporate nonprofit directors by the Code constitutes a mandate that directors must in appropriate circumstances make such reasonable inquiry as ordinary prudent persons would make under similar conditions and directors may not close their eyes to what is going on about them.

Because the missions of for-profit and nonprofit corporations are different, the duty of loyalty is defined somewhat differently. The officers and directors of a for-profit entity are guided by their duty to maximize long-term profit for the benefit of the corporation and the shareholders. A nonprofit's reason for existence, however, is not to generate a profit. Thus, a director's duty of loyalty lies in pursuing or ensuring pursuit of the public or charitable purpose that is the corporation's mission.

As part of the duties of care and loyalty, certain transactions, called conflict of interest transactions, between the company and a director or officer are subject to close scrutiny. A conflict of interest transaction is defined as a transaction with the corporation in which a director or officer of the corporation has a direct or indirect interest. A director or officer has such an interest if, for example, another entity in which the director or officer has a material interest is a party to the transaction or another entity of which the director or officer is a director or officer is a party to the transaction. A conflict of interest transaction is voidable by the corporation, and may be the basis for liability of a director or officer, unless the transaction was fair at the time it was entered into or is approved in accordance with Code § 4832 (4):

"A conflict of interest transaction may be approved if:

(a) The material facts of the transaction and the director's or officer's interest were disclosed or known to the board of directors and the board of directors authorized, approved, or ratified the transaction;[2] or

(b) Approval is obtained from:

(i) The attorney general; or

(ii) A court of record having equity jurisdiction in an action in which the attorney general is joined as a party."

Code § 4832 also provides that a director who votes for, assents to or ratifies a transaction made in violation of the nonprofit corporation statutes and does not comply with standards of conduct established in § 4830 is personally liable to the corporation. Where corporate officers and directors, contrary to their fiduciary duties, do not advance the nonprofit corporation's goals, protect its assets, and ensure that its resources are used to achieve the corporation's purposes, other remedies exist. For example, Code § 4831(a)(2) authorizes dissolution of a nonprofit corporation in a proceeding brought by a percentage of voting members upon proof of one of several grounds, including where "the corporate assets are being wasted or misapplied" or where "the directors or those in control of the corporation have acted, are acting, or will act in a manner that is illegal, oppressive, or fraudulent."

Columbia has long recognized the right of members of a nonprofit corporation to bring the equivalent of a shareholder derivative action against the directors and officers for wasting corporate assets and using corporate assets for personal gain. In *Bourne v. Williams* (Col. Ct. App. 1981), the court held "that members of nonprofit corporations have the same rights in this regard as stockholders of corporations for profit." This right, however, is not effective where, as here, a nonprofit corporation has no members.

---

[2] Under the Revised Model Nonprofit Corporation Act, the approval by the disinterested, informed board of directors of a nonprofit corporation must be made in advance of the transaction. However, Columbia did not adopt the "in advance" language.

Consequently, statutory authority has been given to the Attorney General to act in the public good in enforcing the requirements applicable to nonprofit corporations. The rationale for the statutory authority is that nonprofit corporations, which usually have no participants with a sufficient economic interest to assure oversight, can only be made accountable for their use of assets if there are broad powers of regulation in a state officer. In addition to the provision authorizing an action to dissolve a nonprofit corporation, pursuant to Code § 4811, the Attorney General may bring an action to remove a director who is "engaged in fraudulent or dishonest conduct, or gross abuse of authority or discretion, with respect to the corporation."

Thus, the Attorney General, acting in the public interest, has authority to seek dissolution of a nonprofit corporation that fails to devote its assets to a public, rather than a private interest. Where such a corporation is operated for the private benefit of an individual in contravention of the principles governing nonprofit status, or where the corporation has abandoned its public or charitable purpose, action by the Attorney General and the courts is warranted.

The trial court correctly recognized the central issue in this case: whether CCFS complied with the requirements that a nonprofit corporation fulfill a nonprofit purpose and not be operated for private financial gain. To the extent CCFS was operated for private gain, its assets were misapplied. Thus, the question is whether the undisputed facts demonstrate that CCFS was operated for the private benefit of Ms. Madison, her family, or other corporate insiders.

The Undisputed Facts

Our review of the record leads to the inescapable conclusion that this "nonprofit" was operated for the private gain of Ms. Madison, her family, and other individuals in control of the corporation. The facts demonstrate a consistent pattern of disregard of CCFS as a separate entity from Ms. Madison and of the fundamental nature of a nonprofit corporation.

21

Even based on the figures provided by the corporation, although they are not entirely reconcilable, Ms. Madison not only was paid a substantial salary, but also was regularly awarded bonuses of 50% or more of that salary. Corporate records and corporate memory are ambiguous about the exact amounts so paid, although it is clear several $50,000 bonuses were awarded to her. The corporation's inexact records on this issue simply demonstrate the inattention paid to distributions to Ms. Madison. Although the board attempts to justify her salary and the large bonuses as merited by the success of the program, including the financial success, that argument misses the point. The goal of a nonprofit corporation is not to generate profit; neither is it to reduce its "profit" or excess revenues by increasing operating expenses that enrich corporate insiders. Excess revenue is to be used to further the public or charitable mission of the corporation. We do not imply that a nonprofit corporation cannot reward its officers or board members with salary increases or other compensation if that compensation is reasonable. Although CCFS argues vehemently that it proved that Ms. Madison's salary was reasonable, we find no evidence to support an argument that regular yearly grants of additional compensation of 50% or more of her salary was reasonable. In any event, it is not a question of whether any particular amount was proven to be reasonable or unreasonable. Rather, the cavalier manner in which the corporate board regularly gave its creator, acting executive director and sometime board chair significant "additional compensation" demonstrates to us that CCFS's assets were treated as a ready source of economic benefit to an individual.

Another example of the manner in which the corporate resources were used involves payment for personal expenses. Ms. Madison freely used corporate funds for personal expenses for herself and her family, such as travel to London and Hawaii. In those instances, no one in the corporation apparently questioned the original payment of the expenses by the corporation, and the corporation was never repaid, even though there is no dispute that the trips had no business purpose.

The use of nonprofit corporate revenue for private gain is dramatically exemplified in the real estate and leasing transactions. Twice Ms. Madison informed the board that CCFS needed additional space, then purchased real property meeting that need, and leased that real property to the corporation. She made the second purchase of property later leased to the corporation shortly after CCFS paid her $437,000 in "prorated back rent" on the initial leased property. The "back rent" was based on an inflated number of square feet at a higher rate per square foot than CCFS originally had contracted to pay and after the rate per square foot had already been increased during the term of the lease. Members of the board who approved this payment were unable to explain how this payment could have been in the corporation's interest.

The leasing by the corporation of space owned by Ms. Madison raises significant questions because the record does not indicate any attempt by the board to inquire about other space or compare rental amounts or ascertain Madison's interest in the properties. The increases in rent during the terms of the leases are difficult to justify as being in the interest of CCFS and are totally unjustified in the record before us. Even these decisions, however, pale in comparison to the remarkable act of giving Ms. Madison $437,000 on the basis of "prorated back rent" for which the corporation was clearly not liable. There is no better example of the total disregard exhibited toward the interests of CCFS and the furtherance of its public benefit mission.

The investment of substantial sums in a bank in which Ms. Madison, her family, and a CCFS board member had significant financial interest, and on whose board Ms. Madison and the board member sat, also demonstrates a disregard of the requirements for such transactions. The requirements exist to protect the nonprofit corporation's assets and to avoid insider economic benefit. Once again, those in control of CCFS abandoned their duty to see that these assets were used to further the corporation's public benefit mission.[3]

---

[3] One board member testified he saw nothing wrong with such transactions: "If board members were giving their time serving as volunteers, I think it would be unkind if they had a business and you needed something they had and then not to purchase from them."

These circumstances as well as others demonstrate a failure of those in control of CCFS to ensure adherence to the basic requirement of a nonprofit entity: that it be operated exclusively to serve public rather than private interests, and that its income or assets not be distributed to individuals in control of the entity. CCFS fails the test of whether it was operated as a true nonprofit corporation. The trial court determined that the corporation had abandoned any public or charitable purposes and had pursued private interests. Our independent review of the record fully supports that conclusion.

Business Judgment Rule as a Defense

CCFS argues that the directors' judgment with respect to the challenged financial transactions was insulated from "second-guessing" by the "business judgment rule." Essentially, the corporation argues that decisions by the Board regarding compensation, payment of expenses, investment and leasing are committed to the sound discretion of the board and should not be reviewed by the courts.

Columbia courts, recognizing the business judgment rule in certain circumstances, have followed a noninterventionist policy with regard to most internal corporate matters and have acknowledged that directors have broad management discretion. Where it applies, the business judgment rule is a presumption that corporate directors, when making a business decision, act on an informed basis, in good faith, and with the honest belief that their decision is in the corporation's best interest. The rule does not apply, however, when the director or officer has an interest in the decision, did not actually make a decision, or made an uninformed decision. Based on these criteria, the Attorney General has argued that the actions by the CCFS board in approving various challenged transactions do not qualify for the protection of the business judgment rule.

The rule does not apply to decisions that breach the duty of loyalty. The business judgment rule was developed by the courts concurrently with the duty of care to protect corporate management from liability for mistakes in business judgment. Thus, the duty of care is implicated, not the duty of loyalty. Simply stated, the business judgment rule holds that directors and officers are not liable for honest mistakes or negligent judgment. Directors and officers incur liability only for gross negligence and are not liable simply because their decisions result in an unfavorable outcome for the corporation. Developed to analyze duty of care issues, the business judgment rule is no shelter for directors and officers who breach the duty of loyalty. As explained earlier, a director's duty to ensure that a nonprofit corporation operates to further its public purpose is part of the duty of loyalty.

The business judgment rule is a potential defense in two situations: (1) where officers or directors face personal liability; and (2) where the corporation (generally in a derivative action) seeks to void a decision of or transaction approved by the board. Neither situation is present here. The Attorney General does not seek monetary damages from any member of the board for breach of fiduciary duties. Neither does he seek to set aside or invalidate any particular transaction. Instead, this action is maintained under the Code provision that authorizes the Attorney General to act in the public interest to ensure that a nonprofit corporation is not operated for private gain. Although the business judgment rule is applicable to nonprofit corporations, it has no application to this case. While the rule reflects a sound judicial policy of declining to substitute a court's judgment for that of a corporation's directors when they have acted in good faith and in furtherance of corporate purposes, that policy has no application to CCFS when it abandoned its purpose and pursued private, rather than public, interests.

Conclusion

After careful consideration of the record, we have determined that the trial court was correct in granting summary judgment for the Attorney General, appointing a receiver, and ordering the dissolution of CCFS. Therefore, we affirm the decision of the trial court and remand the case for further proceedings consistent with this opinion.

OFFICE OF THE ATTORNEY GENERAL OF COLUMBIA

NEWS RELEASE NO. 16-2012, JULY 12
ATTORNEY GENERAL ANNOUNCES INTENT TO PROPOSE COLUMBIA
NONPROFIT CORPORATION LEGISLATION

Springfield — Attorney General of Columbia Michael Allen O'Pake today announced his intent to propose legislation relating to Columbia nonprofit corporations.

Background

The American Competitiveness and Corporate Accountability Act of 2002, commonly known as the Sarbanes-Oxley Act, was passed by Congress in response to the corporate and accounting scandals of Enron, World Com, Arthur Andersen, and others. The law, whose purpose is to rebuild public trust in America's corporate sector, requires that publicly traded companies adhere to new governance standards that increase board members' roles in overseeing financial transactions and auditing procedures.

Virtually untouched by Sarbanes-Oxley is the fastest growing sector of the corporate culture, the nonprofit corporation. Explosive growth of the nonprofit sector along with significant expansion into commercial activities have transformed the typical not-for-profit from a charity managing a modest perpetual fund into a modern enterprise subject to the management demands and market forces of a complex business. Columbia, home to thousands of nonprofits, has more than 3,500 with annual revenue in excess of $1 million. The revenue sources of Columbia nonprofits in 2008 were 48% fees and charges, 34% philanthropy, and 18% public funds.

Nonprofits account for a significant portion of the Columbia economy and many of our citizens are dependent on these public mutual benefit organizations. Maintaining the financial strength of these corporations is critical to the State. Financial integrity is essential to the financial soundness of nonprofits. Critch Rating recently wrote, "Nonprofit companies found to have exceptionally weak corporate governance or disclosure practices could face a downgrade in their tax-exempt bond rating or other negative financial rating action, while those with very strong practices might warrant a special or favorable mention in the credit analysis."

Key Provisions

The Columbia Nonprofit Accountability Act is a comprehensive plan for nonprofits with $3 million in assets or $1 million in gross revenue per year. The legislation addresses the certification of financial information; the creation of executive and audit committees; and controls on business transactions with directors and officers.

Certification of Financial Information

The key officers of affected nonprofits (the CEO and CFO) will be required to verify the annual report and related documents. In addition to certifying the financial report is fairly presented, these officers must verify that there are no material omissions or misstatements in the annual report; that they personally have reviewed the nonprofit's internal controls and found them effective; and that any concerns about misstatements, fraud or the internal controls have been disclosed to the nonprofit's audit committee and the external auditors.

Executive and Audit Committees

A nonprofit corporation with a board of directors consisting of 15 or more members will be required to establish an executive committee consisting of at least three directors to facilitate the exercise of effective board oversight.

The required audit committee will be directly responsible for appointment, compensation and oversight of the nonprofit's external and independent accountant who will prepare the annual audit and related financial reports. The audit committee also will be required to establish procedures to receive and review complaints about financial and related affairs, including anonymous complaints from the staff of the nonprofit corporation. The audit committee must include at least one independent director with financial expertise.

The audit committee must meet annually with the external and independent auditor outside the presence of the nonprofit corporation's officers. Finally, the lead partner of the company's auditing firm must be changed at least every five years.

Each member of a nonprofit corporation's audit committee will be required to be an "independent" director. Independence will be defined as not being a member of management and not receiving compensation from the company as a consultant for other professional services (although service on the board may be compensated). A company also will be required to disclose if it has a "financial expert" on the audit committee. If the committee does not have such an expert the company must provide an explanation for its decision. While a company's directors have the right to establish specific qualifications for a "financial expert," the Act will set forth that a company should look to an individual's education and experience as a public accountant, auditor, or principal accounting officer. Key responsibilities of the audit committee are direct control of hiring, setting the compensation for and overseeing the activities of the company's outside auditing firm.

Business Transactions with Directors and Officers

Current Columbia law allows nonprofit corporations to enter into business or financial transactions with directors or officers as long as the transactions are fair and reasonable to the company. Such transactions still will be permitted. However, the Attorney General will have express authority to challenge such transactions, and the burden will be on the corporation to establish fairness and reasonableness based on several factors, including cost and the quality of the services or products being provided.

This rule will apply to transactions with individual directors and officers and to transactions with any entity if a director or officer of the nonprofit corporation is also a director or officer of the other entity. Any director who approves a transaction that is determined not to be fair and reasonable, as well as the director or officer who enters into the transaction with the corporation, will be subject to financial penalties.

A transaction will be presumed to be fair and reasonable if (1) it is approved in advance by the board of directors; (2) all terms of the deal are disclosed to the board in advance; (3) comparability data is obtained and relied upon; and (4) the basis for the board's decision is documented.

For more information, please contact Gary Dimmick at 555.659.5959.

- # -

PT - A
ANSWER 1

To: Luan Wan

From: Applicant

RE: CLEF, Inc. - Corporative Governance Review

Summary

College Loan Equity Fund (CLEF) is a nonprofit student loan organization, whose mission is to help finance the education of a broad range of students. CLEF has a special commitment to providing loans to students in financial need. Although CLEF began as a small family business, it has grown considerably in size and now holds assets of $5 billion. However, its practices have not evolved to keep pace with its growth.

The new CEO is concerned that the five specific practices enumerated below may expose individual directors and the corporation itself to liability. This memo will consider potential liability of individual officers and directors as well as the corporation itself under both existing and proposed law, and suggest modifications that will protect all parties from liability should the new law go into effect. These modifications will try to take into account the CEO's concern that the current culture of the Board may itself be an impediment to compliance. It is likely that the best way to present such changes to avoid resistance from current management will be to frame them in the context of the recent changes to CLEF and recent developments in the law.

1. Engagement of an outside accountant

CLEF currently receives an annual accounting report from Metzger Associates. The principal in Metzger Associates is Sue Metzger, the first cousin of Melvin Metzger who is the founder of CLEF and currently sits on its Board. Metzger Associates has served as CLEF's accountant for the past 13 years. Metzger Associates only charges half as much as a larger accounting firm would, but the reports it provides do not comply with GAAP standards and are not as in-depth as those that financial institutions usually obtain.

In addition, the Board lacks a separate audit committee. It contains no financial experts. Five of the Board members (Metzger and four of his closest friends) are effectively permanent because there is no limit on the number of terms they may serve and they keep being reelected. Three of the Board members must be Presidents of the Humanist Group of Colleges, whose students are a target of CLEF's lending. The rotating directors tend to defer to the directors that have been there longer.

Problems with this practice under existing law

Duty of Loyalty

Directors owe a duty of loyalty to the corporation under current law. Section 4832 of the Columbia Nonprofit Corporation Code prohibits transactions in which a director or officer of the corporation has a direct or indirect interest. Such a transaction can be voided by the corporation and expose the director to liability unless it was fair at the time it was entered into or it was approved by the Board or a committee thereof after a full disclosure of the material facts. In order to approve a conflict of interest transaction, a majority of the directors who have no direct or indirect interest in the transaction must affirmatively vote to approve it. Such a vote removes the voidability and personal liability for the transaction. However, directors must comply with their fiduciary duties in voting. A director who votes in violation of § 4830 (Duty of Care, discussed below) is personally liable to the corporation.

Here, a conflict exists because Melvin's first cousin, Sue, has been benefitting from serving as CLEF's accountant for the past 13 years. This exposes Melvin to liability for approving this transaction and means that the Board can void this year's agreement with her.

Melvin will argue that the transaction is fair because Sue's firm charges much less than a major national firm would. He will also argue that the Board of Directors approved it unanimously at the October 5, 2011 meeting, based on the fact that Sue understands CLEF's culture and goals. He will say that the Board knew that Sue was his cousin when it approved this transaction and it knew the quality of her work because of the history of dealing between the two entities.

This situation is not unlike that in Smith where the company invested substantial sums in a bank in which Emily Madison (the Director and Board Chair of a nonprofit), her family, and another member of the Board had an interest. There, the court held that the transaction demonstrated a disregard for the need to protect the nonprofit's assets and to avoid benefitting insiders. One of the Board members testified that it would have been "unkind" for the nonprofit not to patronize the business of a Board member who was giving her time as a volunteer. However, this logic misses the point highlighted in Smith, which is that the purpose of a nonprofit is not to benefit the individual directors but to accomplish the nonprofit's public purpose.

It is impossible to determine whether this transaction is fair because it does not seem that the Board investigated any other options. It just approved hiring Sue again without discussion. The fact that the Metzger Associate reports are not as detailed or in-depth as what would generally be provided to an entity like CLEF is also a matter of concern. The statement that Sue is "part of the family" suggests that the deal was made to benefit someone that the Board members like, and not because it was in the interest of the organization's mission. Thus, this transaction exposes Melvin Metzger to liability for a conflict of interest and may be voided by the Board, unless the Board voted to approve it.

Here, the Board voted unanimously to approve it. Only Melvin is interested, and thus a disinterested majority approved the transaction. This means that the transaction is probably not voidable and Melvin is not subject to personal liability for a violation of the Duty of Loyalty. However, if the directors approved this transaction in violation of their Duty of Care, they may still be held personally liable, as discussed below.

Duty of Care

Directors of nonprofits owe a duty to the corporation to perform their duties in good faith and in a manner they believe to be in the best interest of the corporation, exercising the care and reasonable inquiry that an ordinarily prudent person would use in a similar situation. If directors exercise such care, then the Business Judgment Rule insulates them from liability for good faith mistakes of judgment or decisions that turn out poorly through no fault of their own. If they are acting in good faith, they may rely on reasonable reports of officers, employees, counsel, or committee of the Board in making their decisions.

In Smith, the court held that the directors violated their duty of care when they leased space from Emily Madison without making any attempt to inquire about other space or compare rental amounts. Again, that situation was more extreme because Ms. Madison changed the lease terms and kept increasing the amount of space being leased. However, the principle is the same: failing to inquire sufficiently into the background and fairness of a transaction can expose directors to personal liability.

Here, it seems that the directors did not live up to their duty of care because they did not consider any alternatives when deciding to retain Metzger Associates once again. The motion was made, Sue's personal qualities were highlighted, and the motion was unanimously approved without discussion. No reports or materials from employees or committees were consulted. In addition, in his interview, Mr. Conway stated that the five directors from academia tend in general to defer to the five directors who have been on the Board longer because the new directors lack the necessary expertise. It is possible that this is an example of such behavior, which would be a violation of the directors' duty of care.

The directors would argue that they should be protected by the Business Judgment Rule because they were acting in good faith in the best interest of CLEF by retaining someone who had loyally served for 12 years as their accountant and whose work they knew. They will say they have no obligation under current law to investigate other alternatives if they are pleased with how things stand.

However, this argument is unlikely to hold up in case of litigation. The court held in Smith that the Business Judgment Rule does not apply where directors have an interest in the transaction or made an uninformed decision. Both factors are true here: Metzger had an interest in the decision and the other directors were uninformed and did not discuss at all the merits of the decision. As stated in § 4832, approving a conflict of interest transaction without fully complying with the duty to make a reasonable inquiry as required by the circumstances is a violation of the Duty of Care and exposes a director to personal liability.

In sum, the directors have acted unreasonably by failing for over a decade to even consider whether Metzger Associates is providing adequate accounting services. The needs of CLEF have changed drastically over time. The directors' duties are not to be kind to Sue but to make sure that its accounting complies with best practices and provides the investors the information they need. It is likely the directors have breached their duty of care. This means they are personally liable to the corporation for damages.

Potential problems under the proposed Columbia Nonprofit Accountability Act

The Columbia Nonprofit Accountability Act will apply to nonprofits with assets of $3 million, and thus CLEF will fall within its purview. Under the proposed CNAA, a nonprofit with a board of 15 or more members must have an audit committee of at least 3 independent directors (i.e. directors with no management role at the corporation or compensated consulting position). It must also include at least one independent director with financial expertise, which should be based on education and experience in the field of accounting. The audit committee will be responsible for hiring an external accounting firm with whom it will meet separate from the rest of the Board at least once a year. It must also have a procedure for receiving complaints about the corporation's finances. Finally, the lead partner of the company's auditing firm must change every five years.

CLEF is clearly not in compliance with any of the required provisions under the proposed CNAA.

Suggested Changes

It seems that CLEF cannot void its contract with Metzger Associates. It could consider breaking its contract and paying damages, but that is probably not in its best interest. However, when the contract is up for renegotiation, the Board should give serious consideration to finding a new accounting firm. The Board should use due care to examine all the options for other firms it could hire and contract with a firm to obtain a full, in-depth analysis of its finances in compliance with GAAP.

Breaking its ties with Metzger Associates will doubtless be difficult and might cause a rift in the Board. One way to approach this is by suggesting that CLEF come into compliance with CNAA now, since the legislation is likely to pass. That provides a more neutral explanation for the need to find a new firm. By setting up an audit committee of independent directors, including a financial expert, CLEF will be able to meet its Duty of Care. It will also benefit from having a financial expert on the Board.

2. Execution of a lease of corporate facilities

Currently, CLEF is leasing space from Center City Realty (CCR), one of whose partners is a Board member of CLEF (as well as a college classmate of Melvin). CLEF also hired Center City to be the general contractor for renovating the facilities.

Problems with this practice under existing law

Duty of Loyalty

Same rule as above.

This also appears to be a conflict of interest transaction under § 4832 because one of the CLEF Board members is a partner of the CCR.

In Smith, the court held that the Duty of Loyalty was breached when a Director purchased property and then leased it back to the corporation. This transaction was particularly problematic because the director charged the corporation "prorated back rent" that it clearly did not owe. In addition, the court noted that Board members could not explain how this transaction was in the corporation's best interest, suggesting that it was truly unfair.

Here, we do not have enough information to evaluate whether or not the transaction is fair, since we do not know how much real estate would have cost if purchased elsewhere. However, the motion was seconded by the interested director (Bernie Baugh). Although the Board then unanimously approved it, this approval is only valid if all the material facts were disclosed, and there is no evidence that they were. If they were, then the transaction will not be voidable since it was approved by a disinterested majority of the Board. If not, then Mr. Baugh would be subject to liability for the transaction and the corporation could void it.

Duty of Care
Same rule as above.

As in Smith, leasing property from a director (or a director's company) without making any attempt to inquire about the rate of property generally or whether other contractors are available to do the work shows a lack of care on the part of the directors. Here, the only information that the Board considered was a Metzger report that this amount was within the facilities budget. This might be evidence of fairness but it is not conclusive. It is still possible that there were much better spaces out there that were cheaper or more suited to CLEF's needs.

In addition, the Business Judgment Rule will provide no protection for the same reasons discussed with respect to point (1).

In conclusion, the failure to make any inquiry into the existence of such spaces constitutes a breach of the Duty of Care that would expose all the directors that approved the transaction in violation of this duty to personal liability.

Potential problems under the proposed Columbia Nonprofit Accountability Act

Under the NCAA, the Attorney General will have the authority to challenge transactions between corporations and their officers and directors, and the burden will be on the corporation to establish fairness and reasonableness based on the cost and quality of services or goods being provided. This rule will apply when a director or officer of a nonprofit is also the director or officer of another entity with which the nonprofit is transacting. Any director who approves an unfair transaction will be subject to financial penalties. Obtaining comparability data is necessary to prevent liability, and the Board must document the basis for its decision.

This transaction would not meet the above requirements because the Board did not obtain comparability data and did not document its decision.

Suggested Changes

This is a long-term lease (ten years), and if the corporation cannot void it, it can consider breaking the lease. Again, however, this might not be in its best interest.

Once the lease expires, however, it should consider all its options before it decides to renew. The Board should thoroughly investigate other available space and consider their cost and suitability to CLEF's needs. It should document all of its findings, disclose all of the findings to the Board, and then the Board should approve the transaction in advance on the basis of the findings.

Again, Bernie may be offended if the corporation decides not to renew its lease. However, presenting this change as a formal necessity under the new law should smooth the transition. It is possible that the lease from Bernie is entirely fair and in the corporation's best interest; but that can only be determined by doing a full investigation into the available options.

3. Purchase of corporate insurance

The CLEF Board just adopted a motion to purchase insurance from a company of which a CLEF Board member is a principal. The insurance will cost 10% less than the premium it would have to pay to renew with its current provider.

Problems with this practice under existing law

Duty of Loyalty

Same rule as above.

This situation is similar to that discussed above, where the company is leasing property from a Board member's company.

Since a director has an interest in the insurance company, the transaction is only permissible if it's fair or if the Board approves it in advance based on full disclosure of the material information.

Here, there is a stronger case that it is fair, because the director is offering a 10% discount for identical coverage. The Board adopted the provision after he stated that offer. It is less likely that this decision will expose the directors to liability because the new policy represents a substantial discount from the previous one. In addition, the motion was approved by the Board after hearing the facts. Although we don't have the numbers of who voted for and against it, it was probably approved by a disinterested majority, since only Mr. Morgan had an interest in it.

Thus, it is unlikely that the Board or CLEF will be liable for this transaction; even though it is a transaction with an insider, it appears to be substantively fair and was adopted after the facts were disclosed to the Board.

Duty of Care

Same rule as above.

Here, the directors at least know that they would be getting the same coverage for less money than their current policy. They can thus make a decent argument that a reasonable person in their circumstances would accept the director's offer to buy identical coverage for 10% less.

In Smith, there is no indication that the directors considered any other options before leasing real estate from a director and investing in her bank.

In contrast, here CLEF had a policy with one insurer and the rates are becoming quite expensive. In response, it has adopted the same coverage at a lower rate. That does not seem to be a breach of the duty of care.

It is unlikely that this decision would expose CLEF or its directors to liability.

Potential problems under the proposed Columbia Nonprofit Accountability Act

This decision would nonetheless be vulnerable under the higher standards of the NCAA. That legislation would require the Board to obtain comparability data and document the basis of its decision, since one of its directors is a principal of the insurance corporation.

Here, although the Board did compare the price of its current policy, it's not clear that constitutes "comparability data." The Attorney General might intend something more robust, such as charts or tables of the standard rate across the industry. In addition, the only documentation of this decision is the Board minutes -- there are no other reports that were put together.

To be safe, the Board should consider obtaining additional data to support this decision and documenting its decision-making process more fully.

4. Guaranty of the mortgage of the former CEO

The Board agreed to guaranty the mortgage of its former CEO, which was made by a bank that one of the Board members is the Vice President of.

Problems with this practice under existing law

Violation of § 4858

Under § 4858, nonprofits are specifically prohibited from guaranteeing the obligation of a director or officer of the corporation. That is because the tax exemptions and other benefits received from the government are to be used only to advance the public purpose of the corporation and not to accrue to the personal benefit of its officers and directors. (Smith)

Here, guaranteeing Mr. Johnson's mortgage is in direct conflict with this provision. Thus, the corporation and the directors that approved it are liable for this transaction.

Duty of Loyalty

Same rule as above.

Here, this transaction is problematic in two ways: first, the Board is guaranteeing the personal loan of a new officer. This seems like a benefit that is accruing solely to a private individual, which is not in line with CLEF's mission. In addition, it might be problematic that the loan is being made by a bank where one of the Board members is Vice President.

In Smith, the court held the company liable for Ms. Madison's practice of using corporate funds for personal expenses for herself and her family, such as vacations to London and Hawaii. Ms. Madison never repaid the company, even though she did not conduct business on these trips.

Here, the directors would argue that the situation is different than in Smith, because CLEF is not just giving money to the new CEO, it is merely lending it to him, and it is doing so in order for him to be able to come and work at CLEF. It will argue that this is part of the package it is negotiating with him and a reasonable form of compensation. Housing is expensive and it is hard to get a mortgage in this climate. If Mr. Johnson cannot find housing, he cannot come and work for CLEF. And in any case, CLEF is unlikely to have to pay any money on the loan -- it is merely serving as a guarantor.

Further, Mr. Johnson will argue that he was not involved in making this decision. The Board decided this in his absence, in order to secure his appointment. He did not make this decision as an interested board member.

In addition, Mr. Niedwicki will argue that there is no conflict of interest because his bank is not engaged in a transaction with CLEF, but with Mr. Johnson, and CLEF was merely a guarantor.

However, as the court stressed in Smith, the bedrock inquiry is whether the nonprofit was operated for a public purpose or rather for private benefit of corporate insiders.

Although it was surely important for the company to secure the appointment of Mr. Johnson, it is hard to see how it was in the company's best interests to guarantee his personal mortgage. This seems like it provided for a large benefit for Mr. Johnson but there is no evidence that this was necessary to secure his appointment or that he was the person most qualified for the job. The fact that Mr. Niedwicki also had an interest in the transaction clouds matters further. The Board also approved this transaction without any information about Mr. Johnson's financial history or the likelihood that he would default on his mortgage.

Thus, it is likely that this transaction constituted a breach of the duty of loyalty by Mr. Johnson (who should have rejected the agreement), Mr. Niedwicki, and the other Board members who approved it.

Duty of Care

Same rule as above.

As stated above, the directors approved this without considering Mr. Johnson's credit history or other factors that would help determine whether this transaction was really in the interest of the company. A reasonable director acting in their circumstances would be unlikely to approve this kind of compensation for a new CEO because it exposed the corporation to liability that did not advance its mission of financing student education.

Thus, it is also likely a breach of the duty of care.

Potential problems under the proposed Columbia Nonprofit Accountability Act

Under the NCAA, the corporation would have to show that this transaction was fair and reasonable. It is unlikely that it would be able to do so, in part because there is no comparability data or documentation of the decision, but also because it is unclear how this decision advanced the corporation's mission to provide funding for student education.

Suggested changes

It is unclear whether CLEF is still the guarantor of Mr. Johnson's mortgage or if the mortgage has been paid off. However, since this transaction violated the directors' duties of loyalty and care, the corporation likely has the power to unwind this transaction under § 4832. If so, it should pursue this option so that the corporation is no longer liable for Mr. Johnson' personal debt, especially since he is no longer the CEO of the corporation and so the corporation is receiving absolutely no benefit from maintaining this liability.

5. Failure to share an internal report with the Board of Directors and with loan fund investors

The Director of Strategic Planning (Wendy Sims) prepared an internal report showing that lucrative white-collar employment is declining and more college graduates are entering secondary and professional school instead. Because of these changes, the default rate for student loans is likely to rise from six percent to thirteen percent of CLEF's portfolio over time, and the loans that are paid back may be in deferral for a longer period of time before being repaid. These changes will alter CLEF's expected revenue in the next few years, which will in turn hinder CLEF's ability to attract investors.

Mr. Johnson (the former CEO) never sent this report to the Board and the report was not disclosed to investors during the last investment offering.

Problems with this practice under existing law

Duty of Care

Same rule as above.

Mr. Johnson likely violated his duty of care to the corporation by failing to share this with the Board. He might argue that this information would be harmful to the business and would decrease investment, and that CLEF needs to keep lending to students to fulfill its mission and thus can't afford to lose investment dollars.

However, by withholding this information from the Board, the CEO was not acting in the corporation's best interest. He was preventing the Board from making fully informed decisions about the health and prospects of CLEF.

He is likely to be personally liable to the corporation for the breach of this duty.

Potential problems under the proposed Columbia Nonprofit Accountability Act
Under the CNAA, the CEO and CFO of a nonprofit will be required to verify the annual report and related publications. This certification must mean that there are no material omissions or misstatements, that the officers have personally reviewed the internal controls, and that any concerns have been disclosed to the audit committee and the external auditors.

Suggested Changes

In order to comply with this provision, Mr. Conway should start by disclosing this information to the Board, especially the independent audit committee. In addition, Mr. Conway must review the current financial statements to ensure that they reflect the information in this report, since it is material to investors. The fact that it is material is evident from the concern expressed at the end of the report that widespread knowledge of this information would prompt disinvestment in CLEF.

Mr. Conway should also take steps to insure that there are internal controls in place to prevent information like this from being covered up such that the corporation releases financial statements to investors that contain material omissions.

Conclusion

A number of current practices, including the retention of an accounting firm that does not comply with GAAP and that is run by the first cousin of a Board member; leasing space from a Board member's company; buying insurance from a Board member's company; and guaranteeing the mortgage of a former CEO; as well as withholding potentially material information from investors, are at least potential violations of certain directors' duties of care and loyalty. Directors may be individually liable for such violations, especially where they voted to approve transactions without using due diligence to evaluate their fairness in advance.

Even where these transactions have been approved by a Board vote relieving individual directors of liability for their conflicts of interest, the tendency of the Board to rubber-stamp so many of these transactions without making significant inquiry into them suggests that the corporation is being run more for the benefit of the insiders than to advance its underlying mission of funding higher education. This mission will be especially ill-served if CLEF continues to withhold important financial information from investors, hindering their ability to make informed decisions about investing in the corporation. Continuing these practices expose the corporation to the possibility that the Attorney General will bring an action to dissolve it based on a finding that it has abandoned its charitable purpose, as in Smith.

Furthermore, if the proposed CNAA is passed, the composition of the Board will have to be altered to include an audit committee, the CEO will have to certify the financial results, and the Board will have to use comparability data and document its decisions whenever there is a conflict of interest transaction.

The corporation should begin making these changes now so that it will be in full compliance when the CNAA is passed.

PT - A
ANSWER 2

To: Luan Wan

From: Applicant:

Re: CLEF Inc.-- Corporate Governance Review

You have asked me to prepare an objective memo to determine whether the following actions of College Loan Equity Fund (CLEF) violate Columbia Law or the Attorney General's proposed requirements:

     1. Engagement of an outside accountant;

     2. Execution of a lease of corporate facilities;

     3. Purchase of corporate insurance;

     4. Guaranty of the mortgage of the former CEO; and

     5. Failure to share an internal report with the Board of Directors and with loan fund investors.

Each action will be analyzed separately below.

Engagement of an outside accountant

The appointment of Metzger Associates as CLEF's accounting firm may violate the Columbia Nonprofit Corporation Code Section 4832. A conflict of interest transaction is a transaction with the corporation in which a director or officer of the corporation has a direct or indirect interest.

Conflict of Interest

According to Conway, CLEF has used a local CPA firm, Metzger Associates, to conduct its financial oversight since close to the inception of the company. The Founder of CLEF, Melville Metzger, is the cousin of the principal for the CPA firm, Sue Metzger. Thus, Melville likely has an indirect conflict of interest as CLEF's transaction with this accounting firm gives him an indirect benefit due to his familial relationship with the principal of the company.

Any conflict of interest transaction is voidable by the corporation and may be the basis for liability of a director of officer, unless the transaction was fair at the time it was entered into or is approved. To be approved, the material facts of the transaction and the director's interest must have been disclosed or known to the board of directors and the board must have authorized, approved or ratified the transaction. Approval by the board requires the affirmative vote of a majority of the directors who have no direct or indirect interest in the transaction. The AG plan would require the approval to occur before the transaction was entered into.

Here, the Board member nominating the renewal of the contract was not Melville. Furthermore, the entire board was aware of Melville's relationship with Sue as the mover stated as much and no objections were made as to the motion and was approved unanimously. It is not clear from the Board Minutes whether Melville voted on this motion. If he did, then he violated his duty of loyalty and can be personally liable under the Columbia Law.

Duty of Care

The Columbia Nonprofit Corporation Code section 4830 requires that directors perform their duties in good faith and in a manner such that she believes to be in the best interests of the nonprofit corporation and its members. This duty requires them to make reasonable inquiries that an ordinarily prudent person in a like position would use under the circumstances.

It appears that the Board of Directors may be in violation of this section of Columbia law by continuing to employ Metzger Associates when they know that the company does not perform the type of audits a corporation like CLEF requires. Indeed, if a national accounting firm is brought in and the company conducts rigorous in-depth SOX type-audits, CLEF will have to pay almost twice of what it is currently paying Metzger. This differential in price should give the Directors notice that they may not be receiving proper services. Further, Metzger Associates does not conform to the Generally Accepted Accounting principles when performing traditional audits. If the accounting firm is not performing appropriate audits then it may be leaving the entity financially exposed to undetected liabilities. On October 2011, the board adopted a motion to reappoint Metzger Associates as CLEF's public accountants for the 13th year. This adoption is likely a breach of their duty of care.

Business Judgment Rule

The Board may be able to assert the Business Judgment Rule as a defense to allegations of breaches of Duty of Care. The Business judgment rule is a presumption that corporate directors, when making a business decision, act on an informed basis, in good faith, and with the honest belief that their decision is in the corporation's best interest. Thus, the directors could argue that they believed to be acting in good faith as they were saving the nonprofit a lot of money by choosing to hire Metzger Accounting. Indeed, the movant of the renewal informed the board that the Accounting firm's principal understood the goals and values of CLEF, and thus they could argue that they believed the company was the best suited for the job, especially since they had employed it for the past 12 years.

However, the rule does not apply when the director or officer has an interest in the decision or did not actually make a decision, or made an uninformed decision. There are concerns that ten of the board members defer to Melville and his friends on the Board when making decisions. If this occurred here, then it is likely that the Business Judgment rule would not apply to protect them because they did not make an informed decision by deferring judgment to possibly interested parties.

Further, the Business Judgment Rule would only apply where the officers or directors face personal liability or where the corporation seeks to void a decision of or transaction approved by the board. Thus, if the Attorney General was suing to dissolve the corporation based on this action, then the Business Judgment rule would be of no defense because it would be inapplicable.

Duty of Care in Relying on Metzger Accounting

Furthermore, the directors may also be liable for passively accepting Metzger's recommendations without inquiry.

So long as the director acts in good faith, after reasonable inquiry when need is indicated by the circumstances and without knowledge that would cause such reliance to be unwarranted, a director shall be entitled to rely on information, opinion, reports or statements, including financial statements presented by independent accountants as to matters the director believes to be within such person's professional or expert competence.

Since there is reason to suspect that Metzger's services are not reliable or based on expert competence as they do not perform traditional accounting measures nor do they use the appropriate accounting methods for an entity the size of CLEF, the CFO and CEO cannot reasonably rely on the accounting firm's statements. Furthermore, while the CFO and the CEO are always present when Metzger presents any report to the Board, according to Cowan the CFO is generally passive in reviewing Metzger's accounting advice. Simply signing off on the accounting firm's advice will subject the CEO, CFO, and Directors to liability because the firm's competence is questionable and thus they may be failing to exercise due care.

Thus, if CLEF continues to employ them and not question or request a change in their practices, they may be liable for choosing an inadequate accounting firm and relying on the firm's recommendations.
Other recommendations regarding finances and accounting

According to the Attorney General's announcement, his proposed regulations would affect nonprofit's with $3 million in assets or $1 million in gross revenue per year. Since CLEF is a multibillion dollar company, the proposal will affect it. The proposal requires a nonprofit with a board consisting of 15 or more members to have an executive committee consisting of at least three directors to facilitate the exercise of effective board oversight. This audit committee would be directly responsible for appointing, compensating, and overseeing the nonprofit's external and independent accountant. The audit committee must include at least one independent director with financial expertise. And the lead partner of the company's auditing firm must be changed at least every five years. Each of its members must be an independent director.

CLEF has a fifteen member board of directors. But, CLEF has no separate audit committee. Thus, per the Attorney General's announcement CLEF will have to create one. Although an informal executive committee composed of Melvin Metzger, Bernie Baugh, and Jane Cross function on behalf of the Board in the interim between quarterly meetings, the committee must be selected by the board. Further, the committee would be directly responsible for the independent accounting firm. Since the firm selected is that owned by Melvin's cousin, he would not be able to serve on the committee because all members must be independent directors. Furthermore, the committee must have at least one member with financial expertise. Currently, the Board does not have many members with financial expertise if any. And those in the de facto auditing committee do not have such experience either. If the Attorney General's proposal is implemented, then CLEF will have to create an auditing committee with new members. Furthermore, the company's auditing team must be changed at least every five years. Thus, Melvin will not be able to stay on the committee every year in perpetuity.

Execution of a lease of corporate facilities

Conflict of interest transactions are subject to close scrutiny. Smith. A director or officer has such an interest if another entity in which the director or officer has a material interest is a party of the transaction of which the director or officer is a director or officer in the party to the transaction.

51

After expanding its services, CLEF doubled its employee numbers and thus found a larger space. CLEF signed a long-term lease for a vacant department store that was remodeled to accommodate the operations of CLEF. A member of the CLEF Board, Bernie Baugh, is a partner in Center City Realty, the company that owns the property and served as the general contractor for the renovation of the facilities. As a partner in Center City Realty, Bernie Baugh has a material interest in the entity and thus has a conflict of interest in the transaction.

The transaction is voidable by the corporation and may be the basis for liability of a director or officer, unless the transaction was fair at the time it was entered into or was approved in accordance with Section 4832. In Smith, the Court looked into whether the record indicates any attempt by the board to inquire about other space or compare rental amounts to ascertain whether the transaction would be fair. The lease and renovation was estimated to cost between $800,000 and 1 million, including all furniture, for a 80,000 square feet and large parking area property. There is no indication that the rates charged for the lease and renovation fall within the market value or that the rates were actually fair.

Here, it appears as though the material facts of the transaction were disclosed but the interests were not disclosed or known to the board of directors who authorized the transaction. Indeed, the board was notified that the property was vacant, had 80,000 square feet, and would cost $10 per square foot, and what the renovation costs were expected to be. The material terms were known by the Board. However, the Board minutes do not indicate that the Board was informed of Baugh's interest in Center City Realty. Thus, it was not validly adopted.

Even if the transaction were fair and was adopted by the nonprofit, Bernie Baugh has violated the Columbia law in that he voted for a transaction in which he had a direct conflict of interest. He seconded MS.Cross's motion to choose the Center City realty's property as CLEF's new space and contractor. Thus, he is personally liable to the corporation.

Duty of Care

Under Columbia Law, The directors must exercise reasonable care that a prudent person in their position would exercise given the circumstances. A failure to act in the best interest of the nonprofit is a violation of Columbia law and subjects the directors to personal liability.

Here, the lease and renovation was estimated to cost between $800,000 and $1 million, including all furniture, for a 80,000 square feet and large parking area property. In Smith, the Court looked into whether the record indicates any attempt by the board to inquire about other space or compare rental amounts to ascertain whether the transaction would be fair. According to their accounting firm, the figures were within the facilities budget adopted earlier by the Board. However, there was no assessment regarding the market value for the property or whether the renovation costs were reasonable. Whether the costs fall within their budget does not help in that the real cost of the property may be substantially lower than the budgeted amount. Since there is no indicating that the directors attempted to inquire as to the fairness of the transaction, the directors may have all breached their duty of care. As mentioned above, the business judgment rule would not protect them as they made the decision uninformed and thus could not have acted in good faith or in best interest of the company. Therefore, this transaction violated Columbia Law.

Attorney General's potential challenge

Furthermore, under the Attorney General's plan, even if the transactions are fair and reasonable, the Attorney General will have express authority to challenge it. Such a challenge will place the burden on the corporation to establish fairness and reasonableness based on several factors, including costs and quality of the services that Cooper City Insurance Consortium will provide. A transaction will be presumed to be fair and reasonable if (1) it is approved in advance by the board of directors; (2) all terms of the deal are disclosed to the board in advance; (3) comparability data is obtained and relied upon; and (4) the basis of the board's decision is documented.

Here, the directors will be unable to meet the presumption because the conflict was not disclosed, no comparability data was obtained and relied upon and the documentation of the vote does not evidence the basis of the decision. Indeed, the motion passed unanimously with no discussions or questions. Thus, if the Attorney general challenges this transaction, the Board will have a heavy burden in showing that the transaction was fair and reasonable. If they fail to meet the burden of proof, then each Director who voted for the transaction will be personally liable to the nonprofit.

Purchase of corporate insurance

Conflict of interest transactions are subject to close scrutiny. Smith. A director or officer has such an interest if another entity in which the director or officer has a material interest is a party of the transaction of which the director or officer is a director or officer in the party to the transaction. The transaction will be valid if all material terms and interest were disclosed to the board and the transaction is fair.

Here, the conversation regarding the insurance premium occurred in front of the entire board. The board was considering renewing their existing insurance policy. Board member John Morgan, a principal in the Cooper City Insurance Consortium, stated he could provide the company with coverage at a price at least 10 percent below the amount quoted for renewal of CLEF's insurance with Intercontinental Insurers. John Morgan has a material interest in the transaction as he was a principal in the Cooper City Insurance Consortium. However, this interest was disclosed to the Directors when he proposed the use of his insurance company. The material terms were disclosed as he said that he could provide the same insurance for at least ten percent below the amount quoted. If the insurance company can in fact provide that amount and did so in fact provide that discounted insurance rate, then the transaction is likely fair as it saves the CLEF money.

The Board's adoption of this insurance policy likely meets Columbia's law requirements to validly adopt a transaction that has a conflict of interest.

However, under the Attorney General's plan, even if the transactions are fair and reasonable, the Attorney General will have express authority to challenge it. Such a challenge will place the burden on the corporation to establish fairness and reasonableness based on several factors, including costs and quality of the services that Cooper City Insurance Consortium will provide. A transaction will be presumed to be fair and reasonable if (1) it is approved in advance by the board of directors; (2) all terms of the deal are disclosed to the board in advance; (3) comparability data is obtained and relied upon; and (4) the basis of the board's decision is documented.

Here, the directors will be unable to meet the presumption because while it was approved by a majority of the board, no comparability data was obtained and relied on. They made the decision based on what John Morgan said the company was willing to do. Thus, the Directors must be able to show that the terms of the contract are fair and reasonable and that the Cooper City Insurance policy is not inferior to the insurance they had with their other provider.

Guaranty of the mortgage of the former CEO

In Smith, the Columbia Supreme Court held that no pecuniary gain can inure to directors or officers of a nonprofit and there can be no direct or indirect distribution of income or profits to them. Under section 4858 of the Code, nonprofits are specifically prohibited from lending money to orguaranteeing the obligation of an officer of the corporation.

On October 19, 2007, Curtis Johnson, the individual CLEF sought as its CEO, requested a mortgage in the amount of $420,000 to purchase a house in Cooper City. Board Member Anthony Niedwicki, Executive Vice President of Cooper City Savings indicated that his bank would make the loan if CLEF would sign as a guarantor. The Board agreed to guaranty Mr. Johnson's mortgage. This guaranty was in direct violation of section 4858 of the code. Further, the guaranty on Johnson's home mortgage is likely an indirect distribution of income in that Johnson would not have accepted the position unless CLEF's securing a mortgage for him was a part of his offer of employment. Officers of nonprofits cannot receive an indirect distribution of income. Thus, the agreement guaranty of the mortgage violated Columbia law.

Furthermore, Code section 4831 (A) (2) authorizes dissolution of a nonprofit corporation in a proceeding brought by a percentage of voting members upon proof that the corporate assets are being wasted or misapplied. If Johnson defaults on his mortgage and CLEF must pay for it, then its voting members may file suit to dissolve CLEF because a payment on suretyship contract would be a waste of the nonprofit's assets.

Failure to share an internal report with the Board of Directors and with loan fund investors

An officer owes the nonprofit a duty of care under Columbia Code section 4830. The director must perform his duties in good faith and in a manner such director believes to be in the best interests of the nonprofit corporation and its members and with such care as an ordinarily prudent person in a like position would use under similar circumstances. Conway found an internal report authored by the director of strategic planning that forecasts changes in the student loan market that could affect the company's liquidity. According to Conway, the report was never sent to the Board by his predecessor and it was not disclosed to potential investors in the last investment offering. This report indicated that the weakness in the white-collar job market nationwide would likely result in CLEF's student loan defaults rising from six to thirteen percent of the annual loan volume. Further, the increase in students applying for graduate school would mean more undergraduate loans would be deferred for the duration of their graduate work, which would lead to a dip in the expected revenue for up to four years. The internal report specifically warns that "such a change in revenue may negatively affect our ability to attract investors in [CLEF's] next offerings." This information is of substantial importance to the Directors and loan fund investors as it will materially affect the decisions they make on behalf of the corporation.

A reasonable officer would have disclosed this information to the board and to the loan fund investors to ensure candor and informed operations of the business. It is likely that the predecessor was interested in keeping this information away from the board and the investors because it hurts the outlook of CLEF's economy. While the former officer would argue that he was acting in his best interest of the nonprofit because the report was speculative or because publication of the report's contents would decrease investor support, these arguments would fail. In Smith, the court unequivocally states that the operation of a nonprofit is for the public good and not for the enrichment of those running it. By ignoring the information and not disclosing it to protect CLEF from losing investors or losing its creditworthiness or other economic credibility, the officer was acting against the main purpose of the nonprofit, which is to serve its public and thus breached his duty of care.

Attorney General Requirements of Reporting

Furthermore, the attorney general's proposal requires that key officers of affected nonprofits (the CEO and CFO) verify the annual report and related documents. The officers must certify that the financial report is fairly presented and that there are no material omission or misstatements in the annual reports. They must also verify that they have personally reviewed the nonprofit's internal controls and found them effective. Any concerns about misstatements or fraud must be disclosed to the nonprofit's audit committee and external auditors.

Here, Cowan's predecessor's actions would be in violation of the attorney general's proposal in that the statement contained a material omission or misstatement in the annual report because it did not include the projections of deferments and defaults that will affect CLEF's cash flow and the information was not disclosed to the Directors.

Going forward, if the Attorney General's proposal is adopted and enforced, the CEO and CFO must verify the annual reports and related documents. They must also certify the fair presentation of the documents. Failure to do so will subject the CFOs and CEOs to personal liability. Since CLEF currently has a deficiency in financial knowledge among its Directors and Officers, it is imperative that the CEO or CFO have such knowledge in order to properly review the financial reports and that a member of the auditing committee have.

Performance Test B

INSTRUCTIONS AND FILE

FLORES V. FALK

FLORES v. FALK

INSTRUCTIONS

1. You will have three hours to complete this session of the examination. This performance test is designed to evaluate your ability to handle a select number of legal authorities in the context of a factual problem involving a client.

2. The problem is set in the fictional State of Columbia, one of the United States.

3. You will have two sets of materials with which to work: a File and a Library.

6. The File contains factual materials about your case. The first document is a memorandum containing the instructions for the tasks you are to complete.

7. The Library contains the legal authorities needed to complete the tasks. The case reports may be real, modified, or written solely for the purpose of this performance test. If the cases appear familiar to you, do not assume that they are precisely the same as you have read before. Read each thoroughly, as if it were new to you. You should assume that cases were decided in the jurisdictions and on the dates shown. In citing cases from the Library, you may use abbreviations and omit page citations.

6. You should concentrate on the materials provided, but you should also bring to bear on the problem your general knowledge of the law. What you have learned in law school and elsewhere provides the general background for analyzing the problem; the File and Library provide the specific materials with which you must work.

7. Although there are no restrictions on how you apportion your time, you should probably allocate at least 90 minutes to reading and organizing before you begin preparing your response.

8. Your response will be graded on its compliance with instructions and on its content, thoroughness, and organization.

Acri and Adams
Methuselah, Columbia

To: Applicant

From: Armond Acri

Date: July 26, 2012

Re: Dalia Flores v. Gary A. Falk

We have filed a legal malpractice action against attorney Gary Falk on behalf of our client Dalia Flores. Falk has filed a demurrer, claiming that the complaint fails to state a cause of action because Dalia was not his client and thus he owed her no duty.

Dalia's mother, María, had requested that Falk prepare a deed making Dalia the joint tenant in María's house. The deed was prepared by Falk and signed by María, but Falk did not record the deed for almost a year. María died before the deed was recorded. Dalia's brother challenged the validity of the deed in the probate of María's estate.

At the conclusion of the probate court proceeding, the court issued a tentative ruling, concluding that the circumstances did not establish that María had an immediate intent to convey the house to Dalia. Falk's failure to record the deed did not itself invalidate the deed. The probate court, however, concluded that Falk did not record the deed because Falk had doubts about Maria's intention to convey title to Dalia.

After the tentative ruling, we settled to avoid a final adverse decision on the merits, and there is no issue of collateral estoppel or issue preclusion. In the settlement, Dalia dropped her claim to exclusive title to the house, but was allowed to stay in the house for two years.

In this case we claim that Falk's professional negligence forced Dalia into settling the case and losing the property.

Please prepare our proposed memorandum of points and authorities in opposition to the demurrer following our attached guidelines. In anticipation of a demurrer, we incorporated into the complaint all the facts indicating professional malpractice. We have nothing to add. Thus, do not argue that we should be given leave to amend the complaint in order to make additional allegations.

LAW OFFICES OF
ACRI AND ADAMS

TO: Attorneys

RE: Persuasive Briefs and Memoranda

To clarify the expectations of the office and to provide guidance to attorneys all persuasive briefs or memoranda such as memoranda of points and authorities to be filed in state court shall conform to the following guidelines.

All of these documents shall contain a Statement of Facts. Select carefully the facts that are pertinent to the legal arguments. The facts must be stated briefly, cogently, and accurately, although emphasis is not improper. The aim of the Statement of Facts is to persuade the tribunal that the facts support our position.

Following the Statement of Facts, the Argument should begin. This office follows the practice of writing carefully crafted subject headings that illustrate the arguments they cover. The argument heading should succinctly summarize the reasons the tribunal should take the position you are advocating. A heading should be a specific application of a rule of law to the facts of the case and not a bare legal or factual conclusion or statement of an abstract principle. For example, IMPROPER: Defendant had sufficient minimum contacts to establish personal jurisdiction. PROPER: A radio station located in the state of Franklin that broadcasts into the state of Columbia, receives revenue from advertisers located in the state of Columbia, and holds its annual meeting in the state of Columbia, has sufficient minimum contacts to allow Columbia courts to assert personal jurisdiction.

The body of each argument should analyze applicable legal authority and persuasively argue how the facts and law support our position. Authority supportive of our position should be emphasized, but contrary authority should generally be cited, addressed in the argument, and explained or distinguished. Do not reserve arguments for reply or supplemental briefs.

Associates should not prepare a table of contents, a table of cases, or the index. These will be prepared after the draft is approved.

SUPERIOR COURT OF THE STATE OF COLUMBIA

FOR THE COUNTY OF ANGELES

Case No. 88888

DALIA FLORES, Plaintiff,   COMPLAINT FOR

vs.   LEGAL MALPRACTICE

GARY A. FALK, Defendant

Plaintiff Dalia Flores alleges for cause of action against Defendant as follows:

1.   Plaintiff is a resident of the County of Angeles, and the daughter of Maria Flores, deceased.

2.   Defendant Gary A. Falk is and was an attorney licensed to practice law in Columbia and was practicing law in Angeles County, Columbia.

3.   On or about October 1, 2007, Defendant was employed by Maria Flores to prepare and record a deed granting to Plaintiff present joint title to certain real property then owned in fee simple by Maria Flores. The property in question was the real property and house located in Angeles County.

4.   Defendant undertook the engagement and represented that he possesses and would exercise that standard of skill, prudence, and diligence that members of the legal profession commonly possess and exercise.

5.   Defendant owed a duty to Plaintiff to exercise said standard of skill, prudence, and diligence by reason of the fact that Plaintiff was the intended beneficiary of the undertaking Defendant agreed to carry out for Maria Flores.

6.   Defendant breached said duty to Plaintiff by failing to timely record and deliver said deed as instructed by Maria Flores.

7.   Maria Flores died on July 15, 2008, at which time Defendant had not carried out the instructions of Maria Flores to record and deliver said deed to Plaintiff. Defendant failed to record the grant deed until August 20, 2008, one month after Maria Flores' death and almost eleven months after the deed was executed and delivered to him.

8.   Due to Defendant's negligence and breaches, Plaintiff's brother Charles Flores was able to challenge Plaintiff's title to the real property and house in a probate

proceeding; and Plaintiff was forced to litigate the rights to the ownership of Maria Flores' property and house, litigation that would have been avoided but for Defendant's negligence in carrying out the instructions given to him.

9. The Estate of Maria Flores was probated under the rules of intestate succession, and during the probate proceedings, in which Plaintiff's title to the real property and residence was challenged, the probate court issued a tentative decision stating that the court intended to rule that Maria Flores did not have the present intent to deliver title to Plaintiff when she delivered the deed to Defendant.

10. In deciding that Maria Flores did not have the present intent to deliver title to Plaintiff when she delivered the deed to Defendant on October 1, 2007, the probate relied upon Defendant's almost eleven-month delay in properly recording the deed.

11. Attached hereto as Exhibit A and incorporated herein as if fully set forth herein as allegations of this complaint is a true copy of said tentative decision of the probate court. By this reference, Plaintiff avers only that the decision said what it said, and does not adopt the findings or conclusions stated therein.

12. As a result of said tentative decision, Plaintiff was forced to enter into a settlement of her rights in the Estate of Maria Flores, which settlement was detrimental to Plaintiff and resulted in the loss of the full value of the real property and residence, which Plaintiff would have received if Defendant had not been negligent in performing his duty to Plaintiff.

13. As a consequence of said breach of duty by Defendant, Plaintiff was deprived of the benefit of the real property and residence that Maria Flores intended should be conveyed to Plaintiff during Maria Flores's lifetime.

14. As a result, the real property and residence that Maria Flores intended to have been conveyed to Plaintiff remained in the Estate of Maria Flores, and, under the rules of intestate succession, the value of the real property and residence was distributed to Maria Flores's three children in equal shares.

15. But for the Defendant's negligence and breach of duty to Plaintiff, the real property and residence would have been conveyed in its entirety to Plaintiff. Said negligence and breach of duty was the actual and proximate cause of Plaintiff's loss.

16. Plaintiff suffered damages as a proximate result of Defendant's negligence, including:

   a. The loss of Plaintiff's right to the entirety of her mother's home; instead of sole ownership of the real property and house, Plaintiff will receive only a one-third share of the value of the property and house, after it is sold;

   b. Attorney's fees paid to Defendant; attorney's fees and costs incurred in the probate case; and other general and special damages as allowed under law.

WHEREFORE, Plaintiff prays for judgment against Defendant as follows:

1. For the value of Plaintiff's loss according to proof.

2. For such other and proper relief as the Court may deem just and proper.

Armond Acri

Armond Acri

Attorney for Plaintiff

EXHIBIT A

Tentative Decision

ESTATE OF MARIA FLORES, Deceased.

Charles Flores, as Administrator and Petitioner v. Dalia Flores, Objector

Super.Ct. No. BP052304. March 26, 2009.

The Superior Court, Angeles County

Kathe Henry, Judge:

For purposes of clarity and not out of any disrespect, the Flores will be referred to by their first names.

Maria Flores (Maria) died on July 15, 2008. Thereafter, Maria's son, Charles Flores (Charles), was appointed personal representative of Maria's estate. Charles has petitioned this court to have decedent's daughter, Dalia Flores (Dalia), transfer to the estate a deed to decedent's home, which allegedly transferred title to Dalia.

Dalia filed objections to the petition. The objections alleged that Maria executed a deed on October 1, 2007, transferring all interest in the residence to a joint tenancy of herself and Dalia; upon Maria's death, title would pass to Dalia exclusively; and after executing the deed, Maria delivered it to Mr. Falk with instructions to have it recorded. The deed was not duly recorded until August 20, 2008, or after Maria's July 15, 2008 death.

We will describe the conflicting evidence in some detail. It is undisputed that in September and October, 2007, Maria was ill with gastric cancer and hospitalized. Maria had surgery on September 17, 2007, and a second one on September 26, 2007. On October 1, 2007, Maria was in the hospital recovering from surgery.

Testimony of Attorney Falk

On or before October 1, 2007, Maria called Gary A. Falk, a lawyer who had helped her in the past, and asked him to come to the hospital. Maria asked that he prepare a "deed as joint tenants." Mr. Falk agreed to do so. When Mr. Falk talked to Maria that day, it was the first time he had spoken to her about a deed of any kind.

Mr. Falk did not recall how much of her medical condition Maria disclosed to him. Mr. Falk did not recall in which hospital they met nor the time of day the meeting occurred. Mr. Falk appeared at the hospital alone. A nurse may have been in the room. Maria was confined to the bed and "seemed to be in a lot of pain." But Mr. Falk testified, "She seemed to have all her wits about her." According to Mr. Falk, she knew who he was and what he was there to do. Mr. Falk did not recall whether he knew she had just had an operation.

Mr. Falk acted as the attorney and notary public in the transaction. Maria signed the deed and signed the notary book. Mr. Falk testified that after he prepared the deed, he "believed Mrs. Flores was under the belief" that he would record the deed immediately. However, after Maria signed the deed, he did not file or record the deed:

"Q. Mr. Falk, just to be clear, the decedent asked you to record that deed?

A. Yes, she did.

Q. And she asked you to record that deed on the date of the execution of the documents?

A. Yes.

Q. October 1st, 2007?

A. Yes.

Q. And after you left the hospital at that time, did you ever receive any other instructions from the decedent regarding not recording the deed?

A. No, I did not."

Mr. Falk testified he did not want to record the deed right away because Maria was in the hospital. Mr. Falk wanted to talk to her after she got out of the hospital to make sure that her wishes remained the same. Mr. Falk explained that he was "just being overly protective of [his] elderly client and because [he had] seen her in the hospital." Mr. Falk believed that when clients were hospitalized, they were a little bit more concerned or worried and "may change their minds upon their release."

"Q. Mr. Falk. If Mrs. Flores asked you to record the deed, why did you wait for over eight months before you did that?

A. I had intended to call her upon her release from the hospital just to make sure that that was - those were still her wishes, and I never did call her.

Q. And so when she called you, she said to you specifically she wanted to make a deed for her daughter, but yet, you didn't just do what she said?

A. Right. I wanted to know what her wishes were. And she said that she wanted her daughter to receive her property once she passed away.

Q. And were you diligent about following her wishes?

A. In terms of seeing that the property was transferred appropriately, I obviously wasn't diligent in recording the deed she had asked me to."

The first time Mr. Falk thought of recording the deed was when Dalia called him in early June, 2008, and asked him for a copy of the recorded deed. Mr. Falk did not recall whether Dalia said Maria was in the hospital or deceased. He thought he was aware Maria's condition had changed for the worse. He did not ask if Maria was incapacitated nor to speak with her. Mr. Falk did not believe that he spoke with Maria after she signed the deed on October 1, 2007.

Thereafter, on June 15, 2008, Mr. Falk sent the documents to the county recorder's office to be recorded. The recorder's office did not record the deed because his notary stamp was smudged and illegible. The rejected deed was received in his office on June 22, 2008. He imprinted another stamp, and he sent the deed back for recordation. [The cover letter resubmitting the deed was dated August 1, 2008.] Maria had died on July 15th.

Testimony of Dalia Flores

Dalia testified that Maria asked her to call Mr. Falk and ask him to come to the hospital. Dalia telephoned Mr. Falk a day or two before October 1, 2007. Dalia related to Mr. Falk that Maria wanted a power of attorney and a "joint tenancy will" prepared.

On October 1st Maria was in pain but "she was herself." Dalia did not recall whether Mr. Falk was there when she arrived or he came in while she was at the hospital. Dalia did not stay in the room during the entire time Mr. Falk was speaking to Maria. Dalia walked out and left them alone but returned. Dalia testified she saw Maria sign the deed or "a paper." And Dalia heard Maria instruct Mr. Falk to record the deed. Dalia also heard Mr. Falk say he would record it.

Prior to the meeting with Mr. Falk, Maria did not disclose to Dalia whom she desired to have title to the residence. Dalia said that she did not tell Mr. Falk whom Maria wanted to receive the house. Dalia told Mr. Falk that Maria wanted to talk to him about a power of attorney and the house. On the evening of October 1st, after Mr. Falk left, Maria told Dalia what she had done and about the deed, with joint title to Dalia. Dalia testified that the first time she saw the deed was when Mr. Falk sent it to her after it had been recorded.

Dalia testified that she lived with Maria all her life. Maria lived in the house with her daughters, Dalia and Brenda, and Brenda's son Donnie. Brenda had suffered a stroke, could not work, and had limited mobility. Maria paid the mortgage, taxes, and insurance on the house until she died; Dalia paid the mortgage on the subject property commencing on July 28, 2008; Dalia and Brenda paid the taxes; they started paying the taxes in November 2008; and Brenda paid the insurance.

Testimony of Charles Flores

Charles, the administrator of the estate, testified that Maria went into the hospital September 16, 2007, and was released October 10, 2007. While Maria was in the hospital, she talked to Charles about the residence. The property initially belonged to both his parents. Because of the bickering between Charles and Dalia, Maria told him that she would rather sell the property and split the money between all the children. After she was released from the hospital, Maria never told Charles that she had given a deed or a joint estate to Dalia.

Testimony of Brenda Flores

Brenda Flores testified concerning a discussion in October 2007 with Maria about the ownership of the house, as follows, "She told me she had signed everything over to Dalia." Maria asked Brenda how she felt about it. Brenda testified that since Dalia was the oldest, she had no problem with it. Brenda added, "Maria knew I still had lots of physical problems, and she didn't want to put that pressure on me." Brenda also noted that Maria could not speak in September for about a week after she had surgery. Maria was under sedation. Brenda knew that Maria was in a lot of pain.

DISCUSSION

The dispositive issue is whether the deed was delivered with a present intent by the grantor to convey title to the property. Delivery to a third person to be recorded is sufficient delivery to the grantee. However, where the grantor has reserved the right to recall the deed, there is no delivery. The concept of delivery involves more than merely physically handing possession of the deed to the grantee or someone on his behalf. The act of delivery must be accompanied with the intent that the deed shall become presently operative as such, that is, must be accompanied with the intent to presently pass title, even though the right to possession and enjoyment may not accrue until some future time. Delivery or absence of delivery of a deed and intention of the grantor to pass title are questions of fact for the trier of fact to be determined upon all the circumstances surrounding the transaction.

There is no issue of Maria's competence or testamentary capacity. Charles, Dalia, and Brenda thought that while Maria was in the hospital, she understood her condition and circumstances, and was in control of her mental faculties.

The facts and circumstances that occurred at or near the time the deed was executed and given to Mr. Falk, however, are in dispute. Mr. Falk and Dalia testified that Maria gave instructions that the deed be recorded. However, this evidence was contradicted in material respects. Charles testified Maria wanted the residence sold with all the children to share equally in the proceeds. Also after allegedly executing the deed, Maria continued to keep control of the property and did not cede control to Dalia. She paid the mortgage, all taxes and insurance. Dalia paid no part of those until after her mother's death.

As stated, delivery with a present intent to convey title is required for a valid transfer. However, recording of the deed is not a requirement for a valid transfer. Falk's failure to record the deed before Maria's death is not grounds to invalidate the deed. Nevertheless, the circumstances of the transaction, which include recordation after Maria's death, are relevant evidence concerning Maria's intent to make a present transfer of the property. Mr. Falk was so concerned about Maria's intentions he took no steps to record the deed she allegedly executed because she was hospitalized when she executed the document. Mr. Falk testified that he felt obligated to retain the document and to talk to decedent after she was released from the hospital so that he could make a further determination that she had made a final decision in connection with the deed. Failing to record the deed is circumstantial supporting evidence of Mr. Falk's doubts about Maria's real intentions concerning the deed. The attorney's delay in recording is significant, relevant evidence in the determination of whether decedent had present intent to convey title of property to her daughter.

Objector Dalia Flores invites the Court to speculate and contends that there would be no issue as to Maria's intent if Falk had recorded the deed as directed by Maria on October 1st, or if Falk had discussed the deed with Maria at any time between October 1st and her death approximately nine months later and then recorded the deed. However, that is not what occurred, and thus is irrelevant.

TENTATIVE DECISION

It is the Court's tentative conclusion that there is sufficient credible evidence to prove that the decedent did not have the intent to deliver the deed to her daughter when she entrusted the deed to her attorney, and that thus the decedent failed to have an immediate present intent to convey the property.

The Court's tentative disposition is to grant the petition and order the Objector to convey the real property back to decedent's estate.

Kathe Henry,

Judge of the Superior Court

JESSICA RUTZICK

Attorney for Defendant

SUPERIOR COURT OF THE STATE OF COLUMBIA

FOR THE COUNTY OF ANGELES

_____

Case No. 88888

DALIA FLORES, Plaintiff,

vs.

GARY A. FALK, Defendant

_____

DEMURRER TO COMPLAINT

MEMORANDUM OF POINTS

AND AUTHORITIES IN

SUPPORT OF DEMURRER

Defendant Gary A. Falk, demurs to the complaint on file herein.

Wherefore, Defendant prays that:

1. This demurrer be sustained and Plaintiff take nothing by her complaint.

2. For costs of suit; and

3. For such other and further relief as the Court deems just and proper.

Jessica Rutzick

Jessica Rutzick

Attorney for Defendant

Defendant's Memorandum of Points and Authorities in Support of Demurrer

In a probate contest between the plaintiff and the executor of her mother's estate, the probate court issued a tentative ruling in which it refused to uphold a deed to her mother's house. The deed, executed prior to her mother's death, would have granted the house to the plaintiff and excluded her brother's and sister's shares. After giving up her claim in the probate court, plaintiff now sues her mother's attorney, who drafted the deed, because he delayed in recording the deed in order to protect his client's interest and to determine if that was her true intent.

Although in limited circumstances a lawyer retained to provide legal services to a grantor may also have a duty to act with due care for the interests of intended third-party beneficiaries, the lawyer's primary duty is to serve and carry out the client's intentions. Where, as here, there is a question as to the client's intent to favor one adult child over another, the lawyer should not be held accountable. Any other conclusion would place the lawyer in an untenable position of divided loyalty.

Statement of Facts

While hospitalized for surgery during October 2007, Maria Flores (the widowed mother of three adult children) summoned her lawyer, Gary Falk, to the hospital and asked him to prepare a deed transferring her residence to one of her daughters, Dalia Flores. Falk prepared a joint tenancy deed; Maria signed the deed. Falk, however, did not send it to the recorder's office until June 2008. The deed was recorded about a month after Maria died.

In a dispute between Maria's son, Charles Flores, as the personal representative of Maria's estate, and Dalia over whether Maria intended a present grant of the house, Falk testified that although Maria signed the deed, he chose not to immediately record the deed, because he was "being overly protective of [his] elderly client and because [he had] seen her in the hospital," and he was "just being overly cautious on [his] own."

The probate court issued a tentative ruling, indicating its intention to grant Charles's petition, resolving the conflicts in the evidence against Dalia. The court found the evidence insufficient to prove that Maria had "an immediate present intent to convey the property" to Dalia, and specifically noted Falk's testimony that he felt obligated to retain the deed until he could talk to Maria after her release from the hospital.

Dalia filed this action against Falk, grounded on the legal conclusions that Falk owed her a duty as a third-party beneficiary of the services Falk rendered to Maria; that he was negligent in failing to record the deed promptly; and that his negligence caused Dalia to lose the property in the probate proceeding. This demurrer challenges those legal allegations.

Argument

> **Where, as Here, a Lawyer Doubts a Client's Intention to Favor a Non-Client, His Primary Duty is to the Client, and the Lawyer Should Not Be Held Accountable to the Non-Client.**

Lucas v. Hamm, Col. Sup. Ct. (1961) held that an attorney who assumes preparation of a testamentary document may incur a duty not only to the testator client, but also to intended beneficiaries, and lack of privity alone does not preclude the testamentary beneficiary from maintaining an action against the attorney.

To prevail in these limited circumstances, the plaintiff must sustain the heavy burden of prevailing on seven factors identified by the Columbia Supreme Court in the Lucas case. These factors are: (1) the extent to which the transaction was intended to affect the plaintiff, (2) the foreseeability of harm to him or her, (3) the degree of certainty that the plaintiff suffered injury, (4) the closeness of the connection between the defendant's conduct and the injury, (5) the policy of preventing future harm, (6) whether the recognition of liability to beneficiaries would impose an undue burden on the profession, and (7) the likelihood that imposition of liability might interfere with the attorney's ethical duties to the client.

Weighing the factors is a question of policy for this court alone to resolve, and thus a demurrer is the proper forum for decision. It is not an issue of fact to be left to a jury.

Here we need but mention a few of the factors that are dispositive. For example, the alleged delay in recording the deed was not the cause of Plaintiff's failure to prevail in the probate court. Rather it was, as found by the probate court, that Maria Flores did not intend delivery of the deed to plaintiff. There is in effect no causal connection between Falk's failure to record the deed and plaintiff's alleged injury. Thus, factor 4 fails.

Similarly, plaintiff has already had a trial on her right to the property. No policy of preventing future harm (factor 5) is served by giving her a second bite at the apple.

Finally the probate tentative decision and Columbia cases dictate that defendant's only duty was one of undivided loyalty to his client. From the circumstances, Defendant was unsure of his client's true intent, and he chose to protect her interest by deferring recordation of the deed. If looking out for his elderly and ill client could expose him to liability to others, it would place an undue burden on the legal profession (factor 6) and would interfere with an attorney's primary ethical duty to his client (factor 7).

Radovich v. Locke, Col. App. Ct. (1995), held that there can be no liability to potential beneficiaries where the testator's true intent is in question. In Radovich, a lawyer prepared a new will for a client naming her husband as a beneficiary but the client died without executing the will. The Court held that as a matter of law the husband could not sue the lawyer for negligent lack of diligence because the "imposition of liability in a case such as this could improperly compromise an attorney's primary duty of undivided loyalty to his or her client, the decedent."

In this case, Falk's duty was to Maria, and his testimony in the probate proceedings shows that he had that duty in mind when he did not immediately record the deed because he was "being overly protective of [his] elderly client." Since it is undisputed that Falk questioned his client's intent to deliver the deed, a rule that imposed on Falk an obligation to act in Dalia's best interests would necessarily result in a breach of Mr. Falk's duty to Maria, a classic example of divided loyalty.

Under these circumstances, Falk did not owe a duty to Dalia, and it follows that Falk's demurrer should be sustained without leave to amend.

JESSICA RUTZICK

Jessica Rutzick

Attorney for Defendant

JULY 2012

California
Bar
Examination

Performance Test B

LIBRARY

FLORES v. FALK

LIBRARY

OSORNIO v. WEINGARTEN
Columbia Court of Appeals (2004)

In <u>Lucas v. Hamm</u>, Col. Sup. Ct. (1961), our Supreme Court rejected the traditional rule that an attorney owed no duty to nonclients. The court held that beneficiaries could sue the attorney whose negligent preparation of a will caused them to lose their testamentary rights, where the attorney's engagement was intended to benefit the nonclient, and the imposition of liability would not place an undue burden upon the legal profession.

Our case is one involving a potential extension of <u>Lucas</u>. Simona Osornio, a nonclient, was the named executor and sole beneficiary under a will executed in 2001 (2001 Will). Because she was care custodian to the testator, a dependent adult, Osornio was a presumptively disqualified donee under Probate Code section 350. After the probate court held that she could not overcome that presumption and thus the bequest to her failed, Osornio filed this action against Saul Weingarten, the attorney who drafted the will on behalf of the testator, for failing to advise the testator of the presumptive disqualification and steps to cure the defect.

In early 2001 the testator, Dora Ellis, retained Weingarten to prepare a new will that would revoke her prior wills and codicils, and name Osornio as the executor and sole beneficiary under Ellis's new will. Osornio was the intended sole beneficiary of Ellis, and she would have received the entire value of Ellis's estate.

Peggy Williams was the beneficiary under Ellis's prior will (1993 Will). Williams filed a petition to probate the 1993 Will. Osornio objected to the Williams petition and filed a separate petition to probate the 2001 Will. The dispute proceeded to trial in the probate court.

The probate court's conclusion after trial was: "Osornio was a care custodian of a dependent adult, Dora Ellis, in September 2001. The provisions of Probate Code section 350 applied, and Osornio has failed to satisfy her burden of rebutting the presumption of undue influence created by Probate Code section 350." The presumption could have been rebutted had the testator obtained a certificate of independent review by another attorney. Failing that, "the Court finds that the evidence before the Court is not sufficient to overcome the presumption that the will executed by Ms. Ellis on September 19, 2001, leaving all her estate to her caretaker, was the product of undue influence."

It is further apparent that, at the time Ellis consulted Weingarten in September 2001, he was aware that Osornio was Ellis's care custodian. In the probate proceeding, both Weingarten and his paralegal, Anne Fingold, testified that Osornio accompanied Ellis to Weingarten's office on September 19, 2001. Fingold testified further that "it appeared to me that Ms. Ellis was dependent on her caretaker, Ms. Osornio."

Osornio's theory of negligence is that Weingarten owed her a duty of care as the testator's intended beneficiary, and that, at the time the will was drawn, Weingarten: (1) failed to advise the testator that her intended beneficiary, Osornio, would be presumptively disqualified unless the testator obtained a certificate of independent review from another attorney, and (2) failed to take appropriate measures to ensure that the testator's wishes were carried out by referring her to counsel to obtain such a certificate.

Weingarten filed a demurrer to the complaint, contending that the complaint failed to state facts sufficient to constitute a cause of action. The trial court sustained the demurrer without leave to amend.

DISCUSSION

In reviewing the propriety of the trial court's sustaining of the demurrer, we, of course, just as the trial court, must accept as true the factual allegations properly pleaded in the complaint.

A demurrer tests the sufficiency of the complaint as a matter of law; as such, it raises only a question of law. While negligence is ordinarily a question of fact, the existence of duty is generally one of law. A demurrer to a negligence claim will properly lie only where the allegations of the complaint fail to disclose the existence of any legal duty owed by the defendant to the plaintiff. Thus, to defeat a demurrer the court looks for facts which, if later proved, would establish a cause of action.

A legal malpractice action is composed of the same elements as any other negligence claim: duty, breach of duty, proximate cause, and damage. Weingarten's demurrer was founded upon the conclusion that Weingarten, as a matter of law, owed no duty to Osornio, a nonclient.

We start with the undisputed proposition that, in Columbia, an attorney's liability for professional negligence does not ordinarily extend beyond the client except in limited circumstances. Indeed, until 1961, Columbia followed the traditional view that an attorney owes a duty of care, and is thus answerable in malpractice, only to the client with whom the attorney stands in privity of contract.

In Lucas, supra, the Supreme Court disapproved of the strict privity requirement. The beneficiaries sued the attorney who drafted the will and codicils in a manner that caused the instruments to fail because they ran afoul of statutory restraints on alienation and the rule against perpetuities. The Court held,

> When an attorney undertakes to fulfill the testamentary instructions of his client, he realistically and in fact assumes a relationship not only with the client but also with the client's intended beneficiaries. The attorney's actions and omissions will affect the success of the client's scheme; and thus the possibility of thwarting the testator's wishes immediately becomes foreseeable. Equally foreseeable is the possibility of injury to an intended beneficiary. In some ways, the beneficiary's interests loom greater than those of the client. After the latter's death, a failure in his testamentary scheme works no practical effect except to deprive his intended beneficiaries of the intended bequests. Only the beneficiaries suffer the real loss. Unless the beneficiary could recover against the attorney in such a case, no one could do so and the social policy of preventing future harm would be frustrated.

The Court held that an attorney's liability to a third person not in privity in a particular case "is a matter of policy and involves the balancing of various factors, among which are (1) the extent to which the transaction was intended to affect the plaintiff, (2) the foreseeability of harm to him, (3) the degree of certainty that the plaintiff suffered injury, (4) the closeness of the connection between the defendant's conduct and the injury suffered, (5) the policy of preventing future harm, (6) whether the recognition of liability would impose an undue burden on the profession, and (7) the likelihood that imposition of liability might interfere with the attorney's ethical duties to the client." (Lucas, supra.)

Applying these factors, the Supreme Court concluded that the attorney owed a duty of care to the beneficiary, even in the absence of privity.

In the near half-century since the Supreme Court decided Lucas, Columbia courts have considered numerous variations of the attorney's potential liability to nonclients. Some instances have involved an attorney's duty of care in the estate planning context, while others have addressed negligence claims by nonclients in other business settings.

It is against the foregoing backdrop concerning questions of the attorney's duty to nonclients that we now address the question on appeal.

Irrespective of the wording of the complaint, it is readily apparent that Osornio alleged that Weingarten breached a duty of care owed to her: Weingarten negligently failed to advise Ellis that the intended beneficiary under her 2001 Will, Osornio, would be presumptively disqualified because of her relationship as Ellis's care custodian. Under this theory, Weingarten was negligent not only by failing to advise Ellis of the consequences of Section 350; he was also negligent in failing to address Osornio's presumptive disqualification by making arrangements to refer Ellis to independent counsel to advise her and to provide a certificate of independent review.

We must now address whether this pleading sufficiently alleges a legal duty owed by Weingarten to the nonclient, Osornio, by balancing of seven factors considered by the Court in Lucas.

1. Transaction Intended to Affect Plaintiff

In the cases finding duties owed to nonclients, the nonclients were the intended beneficiaries of the attorney's work, or were relying on that work, or were to be influenced by it (and the attorney knew or should have known this).

Unquestionably, this factor supports Osornio. Here, there is no doubt that the end and aim of drafting of the 2001 Will was to provide for the passing of Ellis's estate to Osornio.

2. Foreseeability of Harm to Plaintiff

We have no trouble concluding that this factor similarly supports Osornio. It was clearly foreseeable at the time Weingarten drafted the 2001 Will that, if he failed to exercise due care to effectuate the testamentary transfer that Ellis intended upon her death, Osornio would be damaged.

In addition, the 2001 Will was a revocation of Ellis's prior 1993 Will, under which another person, Williams, was beneficiary. Thus a will contest in the probate court was probable. This relevant fact increased the foreseeability of harm to Osornio in the event that there was no certificate of independent review of the 2001 Will. It concomitantly decreased the likelihood that Osornio would be able to meet her heavy burden of proving by clear and convincing evidence that the bequest was not the product of undue influence.

3. Degree of Certainty of Plaintiff's Injury

It is clear that Osornio sustained injury. Although Ellis intended under the 2001 Will that Osornio receive the entire estate, she will receive nothing if she is unable to rebut her presumptive disability under Section 350. Osornio's efforts to rebut the presumption have been unsuccessful. Osornio will sustain the definite injury of being deprived of the estate she would have received, but for her disqualification.

4. Closeness Between Defendant's Conduct and Plaintiff's Injury

We acknowledge that Weingarten's conduct, as alleged in the complaint, does not have the same degree of closeness to Osornio's injury that is found in many of the authorities. This is admittedly not a case, such as Lucas, supra, where there are no possible factors that might break the direct causal connection between the attorney's conduct and the nonclient's damage. Here, the facts may ultimately disclose that it would have been unlikely, for a variety of reasons, that Ellis would have obtained a certificate of independent review, even had Weingarten advised her of the importance of seeking counsel to obtain it.

Under at least one scenario, however, Osornio may be able to establish that, but for Weingarten's failure to advise Ellis and refer her to independent counsel to address Osornio's presumptive disqualification, Osornio would not have been damaged.

It suffices to say that we conclude here that the absence of an extreme closeness between conduct and injury, by itself, should not trump a finding of an attorney's duty to a nonclient in a case that, otherwise applying the remaining six factors, warrants it.

5. Policy of Preventing Future Harm

If testamentary beneficiaries who are presumptively disqualified under Section 350, such as Osornio, are deprived of the right to bring suit against the attorney responsible for the failure of the intended bequest, no one would be able to bring such action. The policy of preventing harm would thus be impaired.

The imposition of duty under the circumstances before us would thus promote public policy. It would encourage the competent practice of law by counsel representing testators, trustors, and other clients making donative transfers to persons presumptively disqualified.

6. Extent of Burden on Profession

An important factor we must consider in evaluating Weingarten's potential duty to Osornio under the facts before us is whether the extension of liability here would "impose an undue burden on the profession."

The existence of statutory limitations on donative transfers to certain classes of people is a matter known to competent estate planning practitioners.

We thus conclude that imposition of duty upon an attorney toward third parties here does not place an undue burden on the profession, particularly when taking into consideration that a contrary conclusion would cause an innocent beneficiary to bear the loss.

7. Interference with the Attorney's Ethical Duties

We find that the imposition of liability here would not result in a situation where the attorney would be faced with conflicting loyalties in representing the client. Imposing liability here does not burden the attorney with concerns that would prevent him from devoting his entire energies to his client's interests. To the contrary, it would encourage attorneys to devote their best professional efforts on behalf of their clients to ensure that transfers of property to particular donees are free from avoidable challenge.

We have balanced the factors that must be considered in evaluating the question of an attorney's potential liability to third parties. As a matter of public policy, we must conclude that Weingarten owed a duty of care to Osornio under the facts as alleged in the complaint.

The judgment is reversed.

RADOVICH v. LOCKE
Columbia Court of Appeals (2005)

The facts material to the issues before us are essentially undisputed. Mio Radovich married Mary Ann Borina (the decedent) in 1967. Shortly before they married, Radovich and Borina signed a form of prenuptial agreement, prepared for Borina by the defendant Law Firm. The agreement stated among other things that each party's property, owned at or acquired after the marriage, should be and remain his or her separate property and that no community property shall exist during the marriage.

In November 1983 Borina executed a will, prepared by the defendant Law Firm, which, after specific gifts to Radovich and others, would give the residue of the estate to two charitable remainder trusts for the ultimate benefit of the Regents of the University of Columbia upon the death of the last to die, of Radovich, Borina's sister, and the sister's husband. Under the trusts, income payments were to be shared among Radovich, the sister, and her husband during their lifetimes.

On June 21, 2001, defendant Locke (an attorney with defendant Law Firm) met with Borina to discuss drafting a new will for her. At the meeting, Locke learned that Borina had been diagnosed as suffering from breast cancer, for which she had received chemotherapy treatments. The purpose of the meeting was to discuss the drafting of a new will under which Radovich was to receive 100% of the testamentary trust income for the rest of his life. Locke did not discuss the new will with Borina at any time after the June 2001 meeting.

Locke declares that "I delivered the proposed new will to Borina on October 8, 2001, for her review and comments. Once this proposed will had been delivered to Borina, it was my understanding that the next move was hers. I could not proceed any further with the preparation of the new will until she communicated to me her comments and whether she was satisfied with its provisions. Moreover, Borina told me she intended to confer with her sister." Locke further declares that Borina "did not communicate with me regarding the draft of the new will prior to her death."

Borina died on December 19, 2001. She had not executed a new will. Ultimately her 1983 will was admitted to probate.

Radovich then brought an action for legal malpractice against Locke and the Law Firm, alleging in his complaint that Locke, individually and as a representative of the Law Firm, had been dilatory and negligent in failing to obtain the decedent's execution of the 2001 draft will. The complaint in the malpractice action alleged that the decedent's estate had been valued at approximately $10 million.

Shortly before trial, Locke and the Law Firm (collectively "Locke") moved successfully for summary judgment concluding that Locke owed no duty to Radovich. This appeal followed.

Review of summary judgment involves pure matters of law, which we review independently.

Radovich asserts that Locke, with knowledge of Borina's life-threatening illness, fell short of the professional standard of skill, prudence, and diligence in two specific respects: by permitting three and one-half months to elapse before delivering a draft will to Borina, and by making no effort, in the more than two months between delivery of the draft and Borina's death, to remind Borina of what she needed to do to execute the will or even to find out whether she wished to execute it.

However, the narrow question framed for the trial court, and for us on independent review, is whether Locke's duty to use professional skill, prudence, and diligence extended beyond his client to an individual who would have benefitted had Locke's client executed a will consistent with the draft he submitted to her, but which she never signed. If Locke owed no such duty to Radovich, then Radovich could not recover from Locke for the asserted breach of the duty.

Lucas v. Hamm, Col. Sup. Ct. (1961) is well known for its development of the modern law of the duty of care owed by a party performing a contract to a plaintiff who is not a party to the contract and, in this sense, is not in privity with the contracting party.

The case before us differs from Lucas v. Hamm in one significant respect: Borina never signed the will Locke drafted. The crux of Lucas was that a will the decedent had signed had been rendered wholly or partially ineffective, at least as to the beneficiaries, by the negligence of the person who had prepared the will. By contrast, the crux of Radovich's claim is that a will potentially beneficial to him had never become effective because of Locke's negligence; Borina had not signed it.

Radovich argues that "every one" of the *Lucas* policy factors supports his position here, citing <u>Osornio v. Weingarten</u>, Col. Ct. App. (2004). However, most of the <u>Lucas</u> factors by no means as clearly militate in favor of a finding of duty here.

The "extent to which the transaction was intended to affect" Radovich depends to some degree on one's perception of the nature of the transaction. In <u>Lucas</u>, the circumstances suggested that the decedent there foresaw a possibility of death within a very short time, within days or even hours, and it may be inferred that he, the decedent there, would need to make and implement a decision without assurance that he would have an opportunity to change his mind. The situation of the decedent in this case was significantly different: although she was aware of her cancer and, inferably, of its lethal potential, no one suggests that in June 2001 she believed her death was so imminent as to be likely to deny her an opportunity to give further thought to her testamentary plan after the will was drafted. Indeed she expressed an intention to discuss the draft with her sister, and it may be inferred that she could reasonably have expected the sister to try to change her mind.

We see both practical and policy reasons for requiring more evidence of commitment than is furnished by a direction to prepare a will containing specified provisions. From a practical standpoint, common experience teaches that potential testators may change their minds more than once after the first meeting. Thus we must, as a policy matter, insist on the clearest manifestation of commitment the circumstances will permit.

By the same token, the "foreseeability of harm" to Radovich, the degree of certainty that he "suffered injury" attributable to Locke's conduct, and the "closeness of the connection" between Locke's conduct and the injury Radovich assertedly suffered, are all significantly less in this case than they would have been in a case, such as <u>Lucas</u>, in which a new testamentary document had been signed by the decedent before she died.

On the other hand, the asserted deficiencies in Locke's performance, if proven, arguably should in some manner be sanctioned as a deterrent to "future harm" in similar circumstances. The strongest argument for Radovich's position is that if the duty of care owed by Locke is not extended to Radovich, in the circumstances of record, Locke will be liable to no one and an opportunity to deter such conduct in the future will be lost. Similar arguments were given substantial, if not dispositive, weight in Lucas.

Countervailing policy considerations are present in this case. The imposition of liability in a case such as this could improperly compromise an attorney's primary duty of undivided loyalty to his or her client, the decedent. Imposition of liability would create an incentive for an attorney to exert pressure on a client to complete and execute estate planning documents summarily and would contravene the attorney's primary responsibility, i.e., to ensure that the proposed estate plan effectuates the client's wishes and also to ensure that the client understands the available options and the legal and practical implications of whatever course of action is ultimately chosen. Where, as here, the extension of that duty to a third party could improperly compromise the lawyer's duty of undivided loyalty by making him the arbiter of a dying client's true intent, the courts simply will not impose that insurmountable burden on the lawyer.

We acknowledge that in the circumstances it would have been professionally appropriate, at least, for Locke to have inquired of the decedent whether she had any questions or wished further assistance in completing the change of testamentary disposition she had discussed with him. But on weighing relevant policy considerations, we conclude that Locke and the Law Firm cannot be held to have owed a duty to Radovich to have done so.

Affirmed.

PT - B

ANSWER 1

Memorandum of Points and Authorities in Opposition to Demurrer

Statement of Facts

Dalia (the plaintiff), Charles, and Brenda Flores are the surviving children of Maria Flores. On or about October 1, 2007, Maria Flores employed the defendant, Gary Falk, to prepare and record a deed granting Dalia Flores joint title to real property that included the family home, so that the property would pass to her as sole owner upon the death of Maria Flores. At the time of her meeting with Mr. Falk, Maria Flores was in the hospital recovering from an operation, but she was alert and aware of what she was doing. She clearly and unambiguously stated to Mr. Falk that he was to both prepare and record a deed in order to affect joint ownership in the family home.

Mr. Falk, however, failed to carry out the direction of Maria Flores, and instead did not attempt to record the deed he had prepared until June 15, 2008. But this attempt to record the deed failed, and the deed was not properly recorded by Mr. Falk until August, 2008, nearly eleven months after he had been instructed to do so. Maria Flores died on July 15, 2008, before Mr. Falk recorded the deed as directed. After the death of Maria Flores, her son Charles was declared the representative of her estate, and he petitioned the probate court to direct Dalia Flores to transfer the deed to Maria's estate for distribution by intestate succession.

Dalia Flores timely objected to Charles' petition, but the probate court issued a tentative ruling against Dalia. The probate court found that Mr. Falk's failure to record the deed in a timely manner was significant evidence in the determination that Maria Flores lacked present intent to convey title to the property to Dalia. As a result of this proceeding, Dalia was forced to settle her dispute with Charles. Instead of receiving sole ownership of the property, as she would have had Mr. Falk followed the direction of Maria Flores, Dalia will now only receive a one third share of the property.

In order to recoup the losses she suffered as a result of Mr. Falk's action, Dalia Flores brought a malpractice suit against Mr. Falk seeking damages. Mr. Falk has responded with a demurrer, claiming that he owed no duty of care to Dalia Flores. Dalia now asks that the court overrule the demurrer.

Argument

In deciding whether to grant or overrule a demurrer, the court must accept as true the factual allegations pleaded in the complaint. Osornio. A demurrer tests the complaint only as a matter of law. In a malpractice claim such as this, a demurrer will properly lie only where the allegations of the complaint fail to disclose the existence of any legal duty owed by the defendant to the plaintiff. This is a difficult standard for defendant to meet, and Mr. Falk is unable to make that showing here.

In a case in which the attorney prepared a deed for the benefit of a third-party, the attorney can be held liable to that third party beneficiary for breach of the duty of care, based on the analysis of the seven Lucas factors.

In Lucas the Columbia Supreme Court made clear that third party beneficiaries of a will could sue the attorney whose negligent preparation caused the intended beneficiary to lose her testamentary rights. This holding has since been expanded to include beneficiaries of other legal documents. Osornio. In deciding whether an attorney should owe a duty to third party beneficiaries, the court promulgated a seven factor balancing test: (1) the extent to which the transaction was intended to affect the plaintiff, (2) the foreseeability of harm to the plaintiff, (3) the degree of certainty that the plaintiff suffered injury, (4) the closeness of the connection between defendant's conduct and the injury suffered, (5) the policy of preventing future harm, (6) whether finding liability would impose an undue burden on the legal profession, and (7) the likelihood that imposing liability would interfere with ethical duties owed to the client. Lucas.

In his demurrer, Mr. Falk addresses only half of these seven factors, specifically ignoring those that favor the plaintiff in this case, while misinterpreting others. The following analysis will indicate that Mr. Falk owed a duty of care to Dalia Flores when he failed to carry out her mother's direction in recording the deed in this case. As a result, the demurrer should be overruled.

Drafting and recording of a deed for the benefit of a third party is a transaction that is clearly intended to benefit that third party because it creates property rights in that third party.

Cases finding duties owed to nonclients often have the nonclient as an intended beneficiary of the attorney's work. Osornio. In that case, as in Lucas the transaction at issue involved a testamentary document. However, it is clear that a deed conveying property to a third party, not represented by the drafting attorney, is intended to affect that third party. The creation of property rights, where none previously existed is a legal effect. Before Maria Flores directed Mr. Falk to draft and record the deed in favor of Dalia, Dalia had a mere expectancy in the property as an heir apparent. Had the deed been effective, which would have been more likely had Mr. Falk done as instructed; Dalia would have obtained sole ownership of the property instead.

Here, as in Osornio this factor "unquestionably" supports Dalia Flores' claim of a legal duty. Mr. Falk's demurrer implicitly acknowledges this by refusing to address it. Radovich, on which Mr. Falk relies heavily in his demurrer, is of no help to him on this factor. There the court was concerned with a lack of commitment to a particular course of action, and found that merely asking a lawyer to draft a will, without executing it was insufficient to show that the transaction was clearly intended to benefit a third party. Here, by contrast, Maria Flores actually executed the deed and conveyed it to Mr. Falk with a direction that it be recorded. This is clear evidence of a commitment and intent to benefit Dalia as a third party.

It is easily foreseeable that failure of a deed purporting to transfer property to a named third party will cause harm to that third party should the deed prove ineffective to transfer title.

As with the previous factor, this factor weighs heavily in favor of Dalia's claim. When Maria Flores employed Mr. Falk, she stated explicitly that Dalia Flores was to be the named beneficiary on the deed. This, without more, would be enough to make harm to Dalia foreseeable in a case where the attorney's failure to exercise due care resulted in the deed being ineffective to transfer title. In this case, however, there is more. Not only did Maria Flores state her intention, but Dalia herself was the one to place the phone call to Mr. Falk in order to ask him to come to the hospital. Thus, Mr. Falk knew of Maria Flores' desire to transfer title to Dalia, and knew exactly who Dalia was.

The fact that this situation involves a deed rather than a will does nothing to make the harm less foreseeable, and this case cannot be distinguished from Osornio and Lucas on this factor. Mr. Falk might claim that a contest to the deed was less foreseeable here than was the will contest in Osornio because in that case there was a prior will that would be probated if the new will was not given effect. However, in this case it should have been apparent to Mr. Falk that a failure of the deed would result in passage of the real property by intestate succession resulting in a much lesser interest in the property for Dalia. Mr. Falk has helped Maria with legal issues in the past and either knew, or should have known, her intestate status.

An injury already suffered, with concrete damages, is a certain injury that weighs heavily in favor of finding a duty to an injured third party beneficiary.

The injury suffered by Dalia in this case is more certain than that suffered by the plaintiff in Osornio. In that case, the litigation over the decedent's will had not concluded, and it was not yet certain that the plaintiff in the malpractice suit would lose, although the outcome appeared likely to be adverse. By comparison, in this case Dalia Flores has already been forced into a settlement agreement with Charles Flores, as a result of the probate court's tentative ruling. She has already agreed to give up sole ownership of the family home that Maria Flores intended to convey to her.

Although Dalia Flores will receive some money as a result of the settlement agreement, it is far less than the full value of the property. Furthermore, the law has long recognized the special and unique nature of real property, for example through a willingness to grant specific performance in land sale contracts. Mere money damages are a poor substitute for the privileges of exclusive ownership in land. This is even more so here, where the real property at issue was a family homestead in which Dalia Flores has spent a great portion of her life, living with and caring for her mother.

Where an attorney's negligent conduct is a substantial factor in a court's decision not to grant a deed legal effect, there is sufficient closeness between the attorney's conduct and the plaintiff's injury to support a legal duty.

Mr. Falk finally turns to the Lucas factors here, at factor four. He claims that this factor weighs against a finding of duty because his failure to record the deed as directed was not the cause of Dalia's failure to prevail in probate court. Rather, he claims that the cause of the probate court's decision was the lack of present intent to convey legal title on the part of Maria Flores. Mr. Falk, however, overstates the required causal relationship between conduct and injury that is necessary in order to impose a duty. The casual relationship in this case is more than sufficient to do so.

Although it is true that in Lucas there was a direct chain of causation, and there were no possible factors that could break the chain between attorney's conduct and the nonclient's injury, the court in Osornio made clear that this is not required. Rather, so long as "at least one scenario" may allow the plaintiff to show that but for the attorney's failure the plaintiff would not have been damaged there is sufficient causation. In this case, alleged, and it must be taken as true for purposes of this motion, that the probate court relied on Mr. Falk's failure to record the deed in a timely manner in concluding that Maria Flores lacked present intent to transfer title.

Thus, Dalia Flores can easily illustrate "one scenario" in which she would not have been harmed but for Mr. Falk's failure to follow simple instructions. Had Mr. Falk done as Maria Flores instructed him to, and had he timely recorded the deed, the probate court would have had no basis for finding a lack of intent to transfer title. In that scenario, Dalia would have prevailed in probate court, and would have suffered no injury. Thus,

93

but for Mr. Falk's failure to timely record, Dalia would have been the sole owner of the real property at issue. That is sufficient to support a legal duty between the attorney and the third-party beneficiary under Osornio.

Preventing attorneys from failing to follow clear and unambiguous directions from clients is prevention of future harm, and supports imposition of a duty to third parties.

This fifth factor of the analysis attempts to determine whether imposing liability on an attorney to a nonclient beneficiary would further the policy of preventing future harm. The courts have long been concerned that if third party beneficiaries are unable to sue the attorney for malpractice, no one will be able to. This is especially true in the context of testamentary transactions, where the client testator is typically dead by the time the attorney's malpractice comes to life. In cases of ordinary contracts and deeds, this interest may be less compelling. In the standard case, the client may very well still be alive and able to sue the attorney when the failure of the deed or contract comes to light.

In this case, however, Maria Flores was in fact dead because Mr. Falk's failure was exposed. Maria Flores is thus unable to bring suit to hold Mr. Falk accountable for his failure, and absent a duty owed to Dalia, as a nonclient beneficiary, Mr. Falk will get away with his misconduct. The courts have imposed this kind of liability in the context of ordinary, nontestamentary contracts, See Osornio, and there is no reason not to do so here.

In arguing that this factor weighs against Dalia's claim, Mr. Falk apparently misunderstands the clear purpose of this analysis. He claims that no policy is served by giving Dalia a second chance to litigate her right to the real property. This is plainly not correct. The future harm that courts seek to avoid here is not any harm to the plaintiff in the case at hand. But rather it is future harm inflicted by Mr. Falk, and other attorneys who neglect their duties, on future nonclient beneficiaries. The courts seek to hold attorneys to account for their actions, so that they will exercise due care in creating legal interests in third parties on behalf of old, dying, or sick clients. That is the situation of this case, and that is the harm to be prevented. Furthermore, Dalia is not litigating here her right to the real property. That was a matter for the probate court. Whether or not Dalia Flores was entitled to the real property that was the subject of the deed Mr. Falk failed to record is only tangentially at issue here. At issue here is Mr. Falk's dereliction of duty in failing to timely record the deed as he was clearly instructed to do.

In Radovich, the court noted that prior cases, such as Lucas had given this factor substantial, if not dispositive weight in the analysis. Here this factor weighs in favor of Dalia, and as such tips the scale significantly in her favor. Although it may not be dispositive in and of itself, it certainly presents a compelling reason to impose liability on Mr. Falk.

Although imposition of a duty of care to nonclients necessarily imposes some burden on the legal profession, that burden is not significant in a case where the attorney failed to follow unambiguous and simple instructions from a client to the detriment of a third party, and the attorney's failure relates to a well-known rule of law.

Although it is not entirely clear from the demurrer, Mr. Falk appears to claim that imposing liability on him, and other attorneys in similar situations, would impose an undue burden not the legal profession because it would require them to defer to the wishes of their clients in situations where the attorney is unsure of the client's true intent. This is an important factor in the analysis, Osornio, and the court must give this factor careful consideration. However, imposing a duty in this case would not lead to a significant burden on the legal profession because of the specific facts at issue here.

In this case, Maria Flores stated to her lawyer, in clear unambiguous language that he was to record the deed with immediate effect. It was clear from the circumstances that Maria intended to convey title in the real property to Dalia, and Mr. Falk had no reasonable basis to doubt this. Although it is certainly true that an attorney has a duty to his client to be sure he understands her actual intent, once a client has expressed that intent in unambiguous terms, the attorney's duty is simply to affect that intent to the best of his abilities. There was no doubt of Maria Flores' legal capacity, either in the probate proceedings or here, and Mr. Falk himself has admitted that Maria appeared lucid and sure of what she was doing when he spoke to her.

In this sort of factual situation it is not burdensome to expect an attorney to carry out the client's intent, and when that intent is clearly to benefit some nonclient third party, as it was here, the attorney should owe a duty of care to that nonclient to affect the client's clear intent. Mr. Falk later claimed, when the issue of his tardy recording came to light, that he was concerned about Maria Flores' "actual intent" because she was in the hospital. He claimed he was being protective, perhaps overprotective, of his elderly client. This, however, is no excuse for failure to do what the client directs. Maria Flores may have been in the hospital, but so long as she was competent and lucid a hospital stay may be just the type of situation in which an attorney's speedy compliance with a client's wishes is especially important. Hospital stays often accompany and always carry a risk of injury or death, and failure to quickly do as a client asks has the serious potential to frustrate the client's intent, as it did in this case.

Furthermore, the reason Mr. Falk's deed failed in this case was the probate court's determination of a lack of present intent to transfer title. As with the statutory limits on donative transfers at issue in Osornio, this is a matter well known to competent attorneys who draft deeds. It is a basic principle of real property law that a deed is ineffective absent delivery accompanied by present intent to convey title. Requiring attorneys who draft deeds to timely record them in order to avoid potential challenges to that intent is not an unreasonable burden on the legal profession.

When there is no reasonable basis to doubt a client's intent, and a deed has already been executed by the client imposing a duty to third party beneficiaries does not pose a significant risk of interference with the attorney's ethical duties to his client.

In expanding attorneys' liability to nonclient third parties, the courts have been concerned with creating a situation in which an attorney's loyalty is torn between the client and the third party. The courts seek to avoid a situation in which an attorney, concerned with avoiding liability to some third party, fails to act in his client's best interest. See Osornio. Mr. Falk claims that is the case here because he was obligated to discern Maria Flores' true intent which, according to Mr. Falk, required him to sit on the deed he had drafted for 11 months without a single communication with his client. This of course prevented him from timely recording the deed, which is now the potential basis for liability to Dalia. Mr. Falk claims that had he timely recorded the deed he would have violated his duty of care and loyalty to Maria Flores. Setting aside for the moment the absurdity of claiming that ignoring a client's direction and making no communications was somehow protecting the client's true interests, there was little danger in this case that any conflict of loyalties would arise.

As mentioned above, Maria Flores' directions were clear, and there was no reasonable basis to doubt her capacity or desire to transfer title to the property to Dalia. Even accepting that in a more ambiguous case there might be some danger of divided loyalties, there was insufficient ambiguity here to pose a significant risk of divided loyalty. All Mr. Falk would have had to do in order to resolve any concerns would be to contact Maria Flores when she left the hospital. Had he contacted her, then recorded the deed after verifying her intent (or even had he not recorded it after learning her true intent was different) he would not have breached any duty to Maria, or to Dalia as a potential third party beneficiary. All that Dalia Flores seeks to impose here is a duty of reasonable care on Mr. Falk. There is no indication from the facts that exercising reasonable care and diligence in recording the deed, even if he double checked Maria Flores' intent, would impose liability to Dalia Flores as a third party beneficiary.

In contrast, in Radovich there was a significant concern that imposing liability to a beneficiary named in a drafted but unexecuted will would cause an attorney to pressure the client into signing the will rapidly, even where the client wanted time to consider and review the document before giving it legal effect. This is easily distinguished from the situation at hand here, where Maria Flores had already executed the deed in question. There is no danger in this case that liability to Dalia Flores would have made Mr. Falk pressure Maria to do something she wasn't ready to; she had already done it.

Mr. Falk also overstates the rule in Radovich. He claims that the case stands for the proposition that there can be no liability to potential beneficiaries where the testator's true intent is in question. This is an overbroad and mistaken reading of the holding. To the contrary, Radovich merely states that the possibility of divided loyalty between a client and a nonclient is a countervailing policy consideration that might outweigh some of the other factors of the Lucas analysis. It certainly does not state that any time a client's intent is unclear that there can be no liability to a third party. Rather it states that the lawyer's duty of undivided loyalty should not be compromised by making him the arbiter of a dying client's true intent. It also does not state that this factor, one of seven, stands alone as the sole arbiter of duties owed to nonclients. Lucas and Osornio make clear that this is careful balancing test. Although some factors may weigh more heavily than others, and the desire to avoid divided liability is certainly a heavy factor, the test requires a consideration of all seven factors, and no single factor is determinative.

In this case there is little risk that an attorney would be subjected to divided loyalty because of the circumstances of the case, but even were that not the case, it would be improper to give this single factor sole consideration in deciding whether to impose liability on Mr. Falk.

Conclusion

This court should only grant Mr. Falk's demurrer if, after accepting all allegations in the complaint as true, it determines that he owed no duty to Dalia Flores as a matter of law. Mr. Falk has failed to make that showing in his demurrer. A careful analysis of all seven of the Lucas factors shows that they weigh in favor of imposing liability on an attorney to a third party beneficiary of a deed when the attorney fails to follow his client's direction to record the deed, and the deed is subsequently found to lack legal effect. The demurrer should be overruled.

PT - B
ANSWER 2

Attorney for Plaintiff

SUPERIOR COURT OF THE STATE OF COLUMBIA

FOR THE COUNTY OF ANGELES

Case No. 88888

DALIA FLORES, Plaintiff,

VS.

GARY A. FALK, Defendant

OPPOSITION TO DEMURRER
MEMORANDUM OF POINTS
AND AUTHORITIES IN
SUPPORT OF DEMURRER

Plaintiff Dalia Flores opposes the demurrer to the complaint on file herein.

Wherefore, Plaintiff prays that:

1. The demurrer be overruled and the case proceed; and

2. For such other and further relief as the Court deems just and proper.

MEMORANDUM OF POINTS AND AUTHORITIES IN OPPOSITION TO THE DEMURRER

I. Statement of Facts

On September 16, 2007 Maria Flores (Maria) was admitted to the hospital. On October 1, 2007, Maria contacted her lawyer, Gary. A Falk (Falk), and asked him to come to the hospital to prepare a deed as "joint tenants" for their family home. There is no question that at this time Maria had her testamentay capacity and competence, and even Falk could tell that she had "all her wits about her." Maria asked Falk to prepare a deed as joint tenants with her and her daughter Dalia Flores (Dalia). Maria did this knowing that she had two other children, Charles and Brenda. Falk prepared the deed and Maria signed the deed and signed the notary book. Falk believed that Mrs. Flores was under the belief that he (Falk) would record the deed immediately. In fact, Maria asked him to record the deed, and asked him to do so on the date that the deed was executed, October 1st, 2007. Maria then told her other daughter Brenda that the property had been transferred through deed to Dalia, believing that what she had asked Falk to do had been done. Brenda has been sick, and lives in the house with Maria, and Dalia, and understood why her mother had done so.

Falk however left the hospital, and did not record the deed as he was asked to do. He did not record the deed even though he had received explicit instructions to record the deed. He never received any contrary instructions from Maria, and he never called her to check in with her. In fact, he did not record the deed until 11 months later, once Maria had passed away. At the time that he finally recorded the deed, he did so without ever checking back in with Maria as he claimed that he intended to do.

Falk claims that he did not want to record the deed right away because Maria was in the hospital and he wanted to talk to her after she got out of the hospital to make sure she still wanted the deed recorded. However, even though Maria left the hospital on October 10th, 2007, just over a week later, Falk did not even contact Maria again, to see what her intentions were, nor did he call her to let her know that he had failed to record the deed. In fact he never spoke with her again.

In June of 2008, Dalia called Falk to ask for a copy of the deed. It was only at this time, that Falk first tried to record the deed. He tried to record the deed at this time even though he had not spoken with Maria since he last had decided not to record the deed. He tried to record the deed for the first time on June 15, 2008. This attempt failed because the notary stamp which he had used was smudged. He then sent the deed back with a new stamp, but this deed was not recorded until August 1, 2008, which was after Maria had passed away on July 15, 2008.

The probate court gave a tentative ruling that, based on this, there was no present intent to transfer the deed and so the deed failed and the property would be probated. As such, the home will be sold and split between Maria's three children instead of going to Maria in fee simple.

Now Falk believes that he is not liable to Dalia, because he claims that he did not have a duty to her.

II. Argument

A demurrer tests the sufficiency of the complaint as a matter of law; as such, it raises only a question of law. In this case, the question is whether Falk had a duty to Dalia, a nonclient. This Court should find that he did owe her a duty as a matter of law as analyzed below.

Lucas v. Hamm held that an attorney who assumes preparation of a testamentary document may incur a duty not only to the testator client, but also to intended beneficiaries, and lack of privity alone does not preclude the testamentary beneficiary from maintaining an action against the attorney. (Lucas). This case has been applied to many other situations and expanded attorney's potential liability to nonclients in other contexts as well as such estate planning context and negligence claims by nonclients in other business settings. (Osornio v. Weingarten). Similarly Lucas should be applied in the case at hand because the case of a joint tenancy deed is similar to a testamentary disposition and it matches the types of cases that Lucas has been expanded to apply to. As such, the Court should analyze the issues in this case under the seven-prong Lucas factors. Because these are factors, and not elements, the plaintiff's failure to meet even a few factors should not be dispositive if the other factors weigh strongly towards finding that there was a duty. When these factors are analyzed, the court will find that it should overrule the Defendant's demurrer.

1. Falk owes a duty to Dalia because Maria's drafting of a deed for joint tenancy with her daughter Dalia, while Maria was sick and expected to pass on soon, is a transaction that is intended to affect the plaintiff.

The court should find that the first Lucas factor weighs in favor of imposing a duty to Dalia on Falk because Dalia was clearly the intended beneficiary of the transaction between Falk and his client Maria.

This first factor for Lucas is that the transaction intended to affect the plaintiff. In the cases finding duties owed to nonclients, the nonclients were the intended beneficiaries of the attorney's work, or were relying on that work, or were to be influenced by it (and the attorney knew or should have known this). (Osornio). In Osornio, the court held that "there is no doubt that the end and aim of drafting of [a will] was to provide for the passing of [the testator's] estate to [the plaintiff]." In Radovich, the court stated that the extent to which the transaction was intended to affect the plaintiff depends to some degree on one's perception of the transaction." The Court stated that in that case, although the testatory was ill, she did not sign the will, so not only had it never actually benefitted him in the first place, the testatory also wanted more time to think about the will and wanted to discuss it with others before signing it. (Radovich) In fact, the court in Radovich stated that the fact that the document had been signed in Lucas and not in Radovich was the "crux" of the case and the key that differentiated the two.

In this case, the deed was for a joint tenancy; the deed would allow for the family home to be passed to Dalia on Maria's death without going through probate. Similar to Osornio, in this case, it is clear that the purpose of the deed was to allow for the property to pass to the Plaintiff and as such she was an intended beneficiary. Maria made it clear that she wanted the deed to be recorded. She intended and likely believed that the deed had been recorded when she asked her attorney to do so. She intended that the property pass to her daughter and she intended that her daughter benefit from this deed. The deed however did not have the effect of making Dalia the intended beneficiary because of Falk's failure to record the deed for 11 months. Defendant attempts to compare the case at hand to Radovich; however, unlike in Radovich, in which the testator had not signed the will and it was not clear that her present intent was to benefit the plaintiff, in this case, the testator signed the deed and believed that her attorney would immediately record the will. She was also in the hospital at this time, possibly after a surgery and so she may have believed that she needed to do this right away. As such, this case is more comparable to Lucas than to Radovich from which it can be distinguished. Falk claims that he was was being protective of Maria because of her health, but he failed to worry about and help the fact that her illness required his actions to ensure her intent to benefit her daughter Dalia after Maria's death.

102

As such, prong one of the Lucas factors has been met.

2. Falk's failure to record the deed until 11 months after he was told to created a foreseeable risk of harm to Dalia because it made it much more likely that she would not be able to show that the deed had properly been delivered after execution.

The court should find that the second Lucas factor weighs in favor of imposing a duty to Dalia on Falk because his failure to record the deed as he stated he would create a foreseeable risk of harm to Dalia.

The second factor of Lucas requires that the harm to plaintiff be foreseeable. (Osornio). This requires that a person in the defendant's position would reasonably be able to tell that they could harm the plaintiff through not exercising due care. In Radovich, the harm was not sufficiently foreseeable because the document purporting to benefit the plaintiff (a will) had not been signed. (Radovich)

In this case, the defendant failed to record a deed that was to transfer a document from a mother of three to only one of her children. If the deed failed, as it did, because of Falk's failure to record, it would clearly create a risk the property would not be disposed of thusly. Defendant failed to take the due care that was required of him, of following the instructions of his client and recorded the deed as she requested or at the very least informing her that he was not going to do so that she could arrange for alternative means of effectuating her intent and benefitting Dalia as Maria wished to do. It made it much more difficult for Dalia to show that she was the true sole owner of the family home and ultimately forced her to settle her claim, because of the difficulty that Falk's failure to exercise due care caused. Unlike in Radovich in which the document had not been signed and so it was not clear that the testator intended to benefit the plaintiff, in this case the deed for joint tenancy with Dalia had been signed and Maria believed it had been recorded. They both believed that the property would be transferred accordingly. This was a foreseeable harm that of which Falk must have been aware.

As such, the second prong of the Lucas factors has been met.

3. The harm that Dalia suffered as a result of Falk's failure to record the deed has a high degree of certainty because had Falk recorded the deed as Maria intended that he do, Dalia would have been the owner of the family home in fee simple absolute upon Maria's death instead of being a 1/3 owner with her two siblings as she is now.

The court should find that the third Lucas factor weighs in favor of imposing a duty to Dalia on Falk because Maria suffered harm that is reasonably certain as a result of Falk's failure to record the deed.

The third factor of Lucas is the degree of certainty that the plaintiff suffered injury. (Osornio; Lucas).

In this case, Dalia would have received the family home in fee simple absolute upon Maria's death had the deed been properly recorded as requested by Maria. However, because the deed was not recorded and so the court could not clearly find that Maria had the requisite intent to transfer at the time the deed was made, the property is probated with the rest of Maria's estate. Because Maria has three children, the property will either be owned by the three of them or will have to be sold. Either way, Dalia will not have a two-thirds interest that Maria intended her to receive. As such, the harm that would be suffered is certain.

Because the harm that was suffered is certain it meets the third factor in the Lucas.

4. Falk's failure to record the deed was closely connected to Dalia's injury because had Falk met his duty and recorded the deed when he was supposed to, Dalia would have received the property on Maria's death and would thus not have been harmed.

The court should find that the fourth Lucas factor weighs in favor of imposing a duty to Dalia on Falk because Falk was an actual cause of the harm that occurred to Dalia.

The fourth Lucas factor is the closeness between Defendant's Conduct and Plaintiff's injury. (Lucas) While there can be different levels of closeness that are sufficient to meet the requirement of this factor, in Osornio, the court held that the "absence of extreme closeness between conduct and injury, by itself should not trump a finding of an attorney's duty to a nonclient in a case that, otherwise applying the remaining six factors, warrants it." (Osornio). In that case, the court stated that in at least one scenario, the plaintiff could establish that, but for the defendant's failure, the plaintiff would not have been damaged.

In this case, had Falk recorded the deed at the time that he had been asked to do so, there would have been a presumption of a valid present intent to transfer the property to Dalia. Had he done so, Dalia would have received the property on Maria's death without any problems. While defendant tries to argue that the non recording of the deed was not a dispositive factor in the Court's decision, he fails to bring to the Court's attention the fact that had the deed been recorded as requested, that action would have been dispositive to the court's decision. Thus, his failure to act was in fact dispositive and was a causal link to the plaintiff's injury. "But for" Falk's failure to record, the Plaintiff would not have been damaged. This closeness is sufficient to satisfy this factor of Lucas, but even if it is not, as Osornio indicates, this should not be dispositive in Defendant's favor. As such, the fourth factor of Lucas is also met by the facts of this case.

5. The Court should impose a duty on Falk because the fifth Lucas factor is met because a nonclient (Dalia) in such a case, is the only person left who can hold the defendant attorney (Falk) liable and the Court should impose liability to deter such future conduct.

The court should find that the fifth Lucas factor weighs in favor of imposing a duty to Dalia on Falk because public policy so requires as there would not be anyone else to hold Falk accountable for his neglect otherwise.

The fifth Lucas factor is the policy of preventing future harm. In Osornio, the court found that the fifth factor of Lucas was met because, "If testamentary beneficiaries who are presumptively disqualified under [a statute] are deprived of the right to bring suit against the attorney responsible for the failure of the intended bequest, no one would be able to bring such an action." (Osornio). The court found that it would thus be a promotion of public policy to impose the duty on the attorney who would otherwise be held unaccountable. (Osornio). Even in Radovich, in which the court did not find that a duty should be imposed on the lawyer, the court found that this element was met because otherwise, the attorney would be liable to no one and an opportunity to deter such conduct in the future will be lost. (Radovich). While this issue is not alone dispositive, it is another factor of Lucas that can weigh towards imposing a duty to a nonclient on the attorney.

In this case, only Dalia, the joint tenant that should have remained after the death of Maria, would feel the real loss. If she is unable to impose liability on Falk, Falk will not be liable to anyone since the only duty Falk claims to have is to his client, who is now deceased, and a client who was counting on him to do as he told her he would, by recording the deed and allowing her property to transfer to her daughter as she requested. In this case, the court should impose a duty on Falk because Falk failed to follow his obligation to his client and now the person who will suffer from his breach is Dalia, who happens to be a nonclient. The Court should impose duty in this case because otherwise there will be no deterrence for such cases in the future.

As such, the fifth Lucas factor for imposing a duty on an attorney is met in this case.

6. A duty should be imposed on Falk as to Dalia because it would not impose an undue burden on the profession to properly deliver and record a deed when the attorney has been asked to do so and to follow a client's explicit instructions.
The court should find that the sixth Lucas factor weighs in favor of imposing a duty to Dalia on Falk because doing so would not impose an undue burden on the legal profession.

The sixth Lucas factor the court should look at to impose a duty on the attorney is the extent of the burden on the profession that such an imposition of duty would cause. (Lucas; Osornio). The courts do not want to "impose an undue burden on the

106

profession." In Osornio, the court held that the existence of statutory limitations on donative transfers to certain classes of people is a matter known by a competent attorney in that field and so the imposition of such a duty would not be an undue burden on the profession.

Similar to Osornio, in this case, is a matter known to most lawyers, especially a lawyer that works with and drafts deeds that there must be a proper delivery to accompany the execution of a deed in order for the deed to be effective. In this case, Falk drafted the deed and then took it with him. He did not leave a copy to be transferred physically, and he did not record the deed as requested. It should have been known to Falk that his failure to record the deed as he was requested to do could cause problems. Furthermore, it would not cause an undue burden on lawyers to effectuate their client's intent when that intent is clearly manifested. Although Falk claims that he had doubts about Maria's present intent to transfer the property, there were no factual indications as to why Falk had these doubts or support these claims. Falk simply stated that he had doubts but not based on any articulable standards. There was nothing uncertain about Maria's request; her request was in fact an explicit instruction that Falk chose to ignore. He was simply second-guessing his client. Furthermore, Falk never did anything to confirm or deny these doubts; rather he decided to record the deed when, one can only assume, he felt like it, 11 months later.

As such, it would not impose an undue burden on the profession to require that an attorney record a deed when he says that he will or ensure that a client's deed is properly delivered when it is requested that it be recorded and so the sixth Lucas factor is also met in favor of imposing a duty on Falk as to Dalia.

7. The imposition of a duty would not interfere with the attorney's ethical duties because in this case it would reinforce the attorney's ethical duties to do as they told their client they would and to ensure that transfers of property to particular donees are carried out as the client wished.

The court should find that the seventh Lucas factor weighs in favor of imposing a duty to Dalia on Falk because doing so would not interfere with Falk's ethical duties as an attorney to his client.

The seventh and final Lucas factor that the court must examine is whether imposition of such a duty would interfere with the attorney's ethical duties. (Lucas; Osornio). The Court is rightfully concerned with creating a situation where the attorney would be faced with conflicting loyalties in representing the client. In Osornio however, the court held that there was no conflict of interest by imposition of a duty on an attorney to a nonclient when it was to "ensure that transfers of property to particular donees are free from avoidable challenges." (Osornio). In contrast, in Radovich, the court stated that pressuring a client into making a decision could create problems by compromising an attorney's primary duty of undivided loyalty to his client. (Radovich.) This was in the context of a will that had not been signed and so the client had not made any decisions yet. The court found that imposing liability in that case could create an incentive for an attorney to exert pressure on a client to complete and execute estate planning documents summarily and would contravene the attorney's primary responsibility. (Radovich).

In this case, there would not be a conflict of interest for Falk between Maria and Dalia, nor would there be a conflict of interest in a future similar situation. This is a case in which a lawyer's client executed a deed that she believed to be a valid transfer of property. The transfer failed because of Falk's failure to record the deed as required to do. Both the client and nonclient have the same goal in this: to have the property rightly transferred. As such, their interests would be aligned. Furthermore, Falk claims that a conflict of interest could arise and that he was looking out for the interest of his client when he didn't record by giving her the opportunity to rethink her decision. However he never even gave her that opportunity. Rather, he neglected to record the document when requested to, and then decided to record it later when it was convenient for him. He never spoke to Maria as he claims he intended to and he never checked to see if transferring the property was her true intent. Finally, this case is not like Radovich in which it was not clear what the client wanted to do and the attorney did not want to

108

pressure her client into making a wrong decision. On the contrary, this case is one in which the client knew exactly what she wanted to do, and the attorney simply thwarted her to the injury of a nonclient. Falk does not want to take responsibility for his failure to record, so the court should impose the duty on him.

As such, the seventh and final Lucas factor weighs in favor of imposing the duty on Falk.

III. Conclusion

In this case all seven Lucas factors weigh in favor of imposing liability on Falk and finding that he did have a duty to Dalia even though she is a nonclient. The failed joint tenancy deed was intended to benefit Dalia, the failure of the deed transfer to be properly executed created a foreseeable risk of harm to Dalia, the harm was reasonably certain, and the harm was connected to the plaintiff's failure to record the deed. Furthermore, imposing liability on Falk would promote public policy since no one else can enforce the duty, it would not be an undue burden on the profession as the duty should have been followed regardless of its actual existence, and imposing a duty is not likely to interfere with the attorney's ethical duties to the client. As such, Plaintiff respectfully requests that the Court overrule the Defendant's demurrer and allow the case to proceed.